Green English

LORETO TODD

Loreto Todd was born in Coalisland, Co Tyrone. She attended Primate Dixon Memorial School, Coalisland, and St Joseph's Convent Grammar School, Donaghmore, before going to Queen's University, Belfast. After graduating, she did voluntary service in West Africa and upon her return registered for a degree in Linguistics in Leeds University. Her doctoral thesis examined patterns in African and Irish English.

Professor Todd is a specialist in Modern English Language and has travelled widely, lecturing and doing fieldwork in places as far apart as the Solomon Islands in the South Pacific and the Sperrin Mountains in Co Tyrone. She has edited three journals, published thirty books and has had many articles, reviews and short papers published. Her publications have also been translated into several different languages. She is currently Director of the Program(me) of World English Research (P.O.W.E.R.).

GREEN ENGLISH

Ireland's Influence on the English Language

Loreto Todd

IRISH BOOKS AND MEDIA

Published in the USA in 1999 by
Irish Books and Media, Inc.
1433 Franklin Avenue East
Minneapolis, Minnesota 55404-2135
First published 1999 by The O'Brien Press, Dublin

ISBN: 0-937702-17-X

Library of Congress Catalog Card Number: 99-61637

2 3 4 5 6 7 8 9 10
99 00 01 02 03 04 05 06 07 08

Layout and design: The O'Brien Press Ltd.
Colour separations: C & A Print Services Ltd., Dublin
Printing: Cox & Wyman Ltd., Reading

In memory of four remarkable people who taught me a great deal
about Ireland and the influence of Green English:

Bernard Nsokika Fonlon, Cameroon
Beatrice Honikman, South Africa
Aiko and John Reinecke, Hawaii

ACKNOWLEDGEMENTS

It would be impossible to list the names of all the people who have contributed to this book. They include the names of family and friends from all
parts of the world and from all walks of life. They moulded my language and
my attitude to languages and they inspired many of the views expressed in
Green English.

I should also like to thank some of my more formal teachers: Sister Mary
Brogán, a native Irish speaker, who inspired my love of Irish Gaelic; the late
Professor John Braidwood, who lectured on Old English and taught me to
treat dialects of English with the same respect that one should pay to any
mother tongue; Professor A.N. Jeffares, whose enthusiasm for Irish Literature is impossible to resist; and Professor John Spencer, who helped to fos-
ter my interest in World Englishes.

I should finally like to express my gratitude to Susan Houlden for her
editorial contribution, to Deasúin FitzGerald for his close reading of the
text, to the Todds and the McCauslands for their support and to Dr Mary
Penrith for her painstaking proofreading and her uncompromising pursuit
of accuracy.

SOURCES

Green English makes considerable use of quotation, both poetry and prose. I have left these in their original form because they are often perfect distillations of 'what oft was thought but ne'er so well expressed'. Grateful acknowledgement is paid to Heather Elliott (*Contemporary Women Writers in the North of Ireland*); Seamus Heaney ('North', *Over Nine Waves*, Faber and Faber); John Hewitt ('Ireland', *Collected Poems*, Macgibbon and Kee); Morris Fraser (*Children in Conflict*, Penguin); Patrick Kavanagh ('Who killed James Joyce?', *Presences*, Chatto and Windus/The Gallery Press and the Trustees of the Estate of Patrick Kavanagh); Frederick Ludowyk (*Ozwords*, Australian National University); Magnus Magnusson and Hermann Pålsson (*The Vinland Sagas*, Penguin); Frances Mulloy (*No Mate for the Magpie*, Virago Press); John Montague ('A Grafted Tongue', Faber and Faber/The Gallery Press); Paul Muldoon ('The Lass of Aughrim', Faber and Faber); Tom Paulin (*A New Look at the Language Question*, Field Day Theatre Company Ltd.); Barbara Strang (*A History of English*, Methuen); W.B. Yeats (from 'Easter 1916', *Poems of W.B. Yeats: a new selection*, Macmillan/Yeats' Estate); J.C. Wells (*Accents of English*, Cambridge University Press) and to all the other writers to whom I refer.

Every reasonable effort has been made to contact the copyright holders of material reproduced in this book. If any involuntary infringement of copyright has occurred, sincere apologies are offered and the owners of such copyright are requested to contact the publishers.

CONTENTS

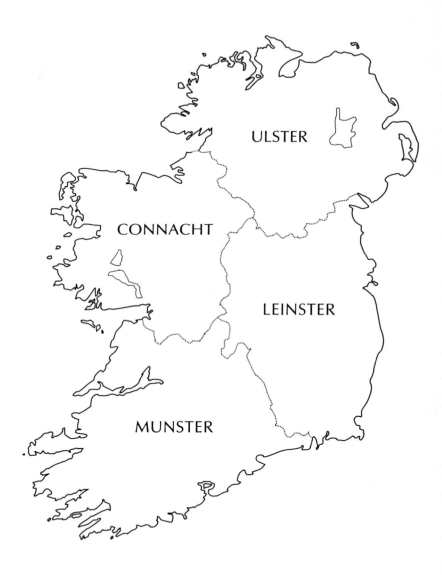

ULSTER

CONNACHT

LEINSTER

MUNSTER

The Provinces of Ireland

The Counties of Ireland

CHAPTER ONE

The Lore of the Land

We are not native here or anywhere.
We are the keltic wave that broke over Europe,
and ran up this bleak beach among these stones:
but when the tide ebbed, were left stranded here
in crevices, and ledge-protected pools
that have grown salter with the drying up
of the great common flow that kept us sweet
with great cold draughts from deep down in the ocean.

(John Hewitt, 1907–87, 'Ireland')

Almost a thousand years before Christopher Columbus travelled to the Americas, the Irish had their Immrama, their voyages of discovery. Saints like Brendan and princes like Mael Dún climbed into small boats and journeyed deep into the human psyche. In these Irish odysseys, they battled with the winds and the waves of the physical world to encounter lands of fantasy where the laws of nature were suspended and human beings were bounded only by the limits of their imagination.

The reader of this book is like a modern *Iomramhach*, a voyager. We will journey through time and space as we look for the source, not of a great physical river like the Niger, but of the island's other language, English – the imposed language, that has become the mother tongue of the majority of Irish people. We will trace its earliest trickle in the first millennium after Christ. We will then follow its rapid growth in the twelfth and thirteenth centuries. We will explore why its flow was subsequently reduced so that it seemed about to disappear as completely as the other Germanic dialects spoken by the

Vikings. And we will observe its renewed power as it grew, spread and carried all before it until it almost swamped the Gaelic system. Almost but not quite. For we shall also see that, in Ireland, the river of English followed channels and courses that had already been established by Gaelic. We are calling this new confluence 'Green English' and we will show that it has spread not only through Ireland but throughout the world, wherever Irish people have migrated. Aspects of it, we will suggest, can be found even in Standard British English. The English Planters tried to remake the Irish 'in their image and likeness', and the Irish 'made haste to return the compliment'.

Green English examines not only how and when the English language became established in Ireland, almost ousting Irish Gaelic. It explores the reasons why this particular variety of English became such a viable medium for creative writing that Ireland can claim to have produced literature in English earlier than Chaucer, so often called the 'father of English Literature'; it examines why the influence of Irish English was carried around the world; and suggests that, although the virtual loss of an ancestral mother tongue may have affected Ireland's psyche, the 'loss' may have been balanced by 'abundant recompense'.

> *...That time is past,*
> *And all its aching joys are now no more,*
> *And all its dizzy raptures. Nor for this*
> *Faint I, nor mourn nor murmur; other gifts*
> *Have followed; for such loss, I would believe,*
> *Abundant recompense.*
>
> (William Wordsworth, 1770–1850, 'Tintern Abbey')

The first coming

Our knowledge of who the first Irish people were and where they came from is limited. If *Homo sapiens* has walked this planet for over two million years, then the people who gave rise to the Irish are a very young branch of the human family. The evidence we have comes from a combination of three main sources. First, there are archaeological relics. These are reinforced by writings – runic, Irish, Latin, French and English. And lastly, we have the oral traditions, which provide a rich mine of myth and legend, fact and fantasy.

> In James Michener's *Hawaii*, the value and accuracy of oral traditions are stressed. He, like many other researchers, discovered that non-literate people often preserve their histories in narrative form. Such narratives may not be as chronologically precise as Caesar's *Gallic Wars* but they have been shown to be both factual and reliable.

It seems likely that the first bands of settlers arrived in what is now County Antrim about six thousand years before the birth of Christ. These people were probably hunters and gatherers who may have walked across the land bridge that, at the time, joined Scotland to Northern Ireland. We can only speculate about these early settlers. They may have been short and dark; and they may have helped to give rise to the legends of the 'little people' who may once have been cave dwellers. We don't know what language or languages these ancient Irish spoke. Their bones and the tools they used can tell us something about their lifestyle, but they tell us nothing of their communication system. We can say with confidence, however, that they had a language as complex and as inventive as any other. It is equally probable that they had an oral literature because all human groups, irrespective of the poverty of their surroundings or their social conditions, have at least two things in common: they all speak a highly complex language; and they all feel the need to preserve their traditions in a stylised form of language that is rhythmic and structured. In other words, they have a literature. But whatever these early Irish men and women treasured has disappeared. We have lost forever the storehouse of this ancient knowledge and wisdom.

Three thousand years later, a second group of incomers probably reached Ireland by sea. These people were farmers and skilled builders. They tilled the land and they made pottery. Of most interest, perhaps, was their preoccupation with the dead and with the afterlife. The megalithic stone tombs they built remind the visitor of the circle of stones at Stonehenge in England or of the pyramid tombs of the Egyptians and Mayans. Unlike modern people, the builders of tomb monuments in all continents lavished more time, thought and energy on the dead than they did on the living. Three millennia before the birth of Christ, many societies constructed edifices that seem to have links with astronomy. The tombs in the Boyne valley in Ireland – a name that will recur in our story – are linked with the winter solstice; Stonehenge in England with the summer solstice; the Giza pyramids in Egypt seem to be lined up with the belt of the constellation Orion; and the builders of the stepped pyramids in the Americas had a knowledge of the calendar that is at least the equal of the ones we regularly use today. Our pre-Christian, Irish ancestors, like all human ancestors, had an attitude towards the dead that we can only guess at. We see both respect for the dead and belief in an afterlife in all of the places mentioned and we see it in every single country where relics remain. A sobering thought for people who glory in European advances is that an Aborigine woman was respectfully cremated near the shores of Lake Mungo in Australia over twenty-seven thousand years ago.

The early Celts

The Celts began to be significant in Europe about 600 years before the birth of Christ. They were excellent warriors, skilled in many crafts and, at one time, they were found from the Black Sea in the East to the western-most islands of Ireland. We do not have early records of their language, although the Greek historian, Diodorus Siculus (90–21 BC), who was a contemporary of Julius Caesar, provides a few interesting comments. In his 40-volume history of the world, *Bibliotecha Historica* (Historical Library), he refers to the 'deep', 'harsh' voices of the Celts and goes on to say:

> *In conversation they use few words and speak in riddles, for the most part hinting at things and leaving a great deal to be understood.*

It is not necessarily the case that a non-Celtic historian would describe the Celtic language accurately. However, the 'l' sounds (or the alveolar lateral fricatives, if you prefer technical precision) that still occur in Welsh **Llangollen** or Irish **ghlan** might well have sounded 'harsh' to a speaker whose mother tongue did not use them. And many of the answers I have recorded to apparently straight questions in Ireland suggest that Diodorus Siculus knew his Celts well! I am thinking of such dialogues as:

Q: *Was he fat?*
A: *Well now, he could roll faster than he could walk.* (i.e. 'yes')
Q: *Did she miss it by much?*
A: *Well, an inch is a deal* (a lot) *in a man's nose.* (i.e. 'yes, by about an inch')

The Irish Celts almost certainly intermarried with the people they found in Ireland, the descendants of the dolmen-building farmers and of the earlier hunters from Scotland. Invaders rarely, if ever, kill off all the women, and the children of such unions often express the stories of their mothers in the languages of their fathers.

Soon after the arrival of the Celts, we begin to find records of language. At first, the records are **runic**, that is, they are lines carved in wood and the patterns of these lines are roughly equivalent to the letters of the alphabet. At the time, very few people could read and so the runes, which resemble a modern barcode, were thought to have magical properties. It is interesting that the modern Irish word *rún* still means 'secret', and the English verbs *write* and *read* used to mean 'carve' and 'solve the riddle of the runes' respectively.

> Ogham is the name usually given to an early Irish runic or linear script that has been found on over 300 stones in Ireland, Wales, England, Scotland and the Isle of Man. A simple form involves four groups of strokes arranged along a horizontal line, such as:

The written word

From the fifth century on, Irish Christianity produced clerics, poets and scholars capable of writing in and translating into Latin and Irish Gaelic. It is likely that many of the religious – both women and men – who travelled throughout Europe spreading the Celtic brand of Christianity were multilingual. There are early Irish saints buried in most western European countries. St Dymphna was buried near Antwerp in Belgium in the seventh century and there is evidence that Irish hermits lived and died in Iceland from the eighth century.

> *Irish anchorites were the first to settle in Iceland.*
> (Magnus Magnusson and Hermann Pålsson, *The Vinland Sagas: The Norse Discovery of America*, 1965)

Contacts with England

It is very possible that many of the Irish saints who lived in England spoke a form of English. St Aidan, for example, went to Northumbria at the request of King Oswald and helped to establish churches and monasteries throughout the north-east of England. His life in England is described by the Venerable Bede (673–735), who is reputed to have been translating the Lord's Prayer into English on his deathbed. Bede comments on Aidan's goodness and humility, his love of prayer and of scholarship. We know that Aidan introduced the practice of fasting until 3 p.m. on Wednesdays and Fridays, except during the forty days after Easter. We know about the noblemen he rebuked, about the women to whom he showed kindness, and about the people, like Utta, for whom he worked miracles. Unfortunately, Bede does not offer any insights into Aidan's use of language. We do know, however, that many monks and nuns left the north of England both before and after the Synod of Whitby in AD 663, and settled in Ireland, where they could continue to practise Celtic, rather than Roman, Christianity. It is possible that some of these Christians also continued to speak English in Ireland, although it is more likely that they used Latin or Irish.

The Synod of Whitby was held to decide whether England should follow the Celtic form of Christianity, including its method of calculating Easter, or the Roman form, practised throughout Europe. Whitby decided in favour of Rome but Barbara Strang's claim is worth quoting. In *A History of English* (1974: 358), she says:

Because the Roman missionaries arrived first in time, and their party prevailed in the end, it is often supposed that the Celtic mission was no more than a peripheral episode. From the point of view of religious history, this is almost certainly a mistake; without the Celts Wilfrid [a Northumbrian aristocratic priest who supported the Roman cause] *might not have had a church to be prince of. For linguistic history it is misleading in the extreme, since the generation in which the Northumbrian Church led in religion and scholarship is crucial for the establishment of the tradition of writing English. OE* [Old English] *orthography can better be explained as deriving directly from Irish traditions, and only indirectly from their source in the writing of Latin, than directly from Latin.*

A timeline

We can supplement our meagre knowledge of the past by looking closely at almost any modern map of Ireland. It provides a timeline that allows us to trace part of Ireland's story. The very name of the country, Ireland (**Éire**+land), indicates a linguistic and cultural grafting that is part of our heritage. We may have lost our ability to distinguish placenames that predated the Celtic invaders but we can easily pick out Irish Gaelic names. Some, like Ballygawley (the town of the foreigners), relate to settlements; some are linked to glens or plains, woods or islands; and some have immortalised Ireland's long history of battles.

Settlement	Current name	Irish source	Original meaning
baile = town	Ballynadolly	baile na dtulach	town of the little hills
gráig = village	Graigeen	gráig + ín	little village

Topography	Current name	Irish source	Original meaning
abhainn = river	Owenmore	abhainn mór	big river
clár = plain	Co. Clare	clár	plain
coill = wood	Kerrykyle	ceithre coill	four woods
gleann = glen	Glenamaddy	gleann na madaidhe	glen of the dogs
inis = island	Inishfree	inis fraoch	heather island
magh = plain	Macosquin	magh cosgrain	Cosgran's plain
oileán = island	Illaunfadda	oileán fada	long island
réidh = plain	Readoty	réidh doighte	burnt plain
tobar = well	Toberbilly	tobar bile	well of the old tree

Battles	Current name	Irish source	Original meaning
ár = slaughter	Drumar	drum áir	ridge of slaughter
corp = corpse	Meenagorp	mín na gcorp	mountain top of the corpses
ruaig = rout	Ballynarooga	baile na ruaige	town of the rout

If we look a little more closely at the Gaelic names, we can detect the early struggle between ancient Druidic beliefs and the new Christian culture. The fairies and the pookas give way to the churches and the crosses. Indeed, one of Belfast's best-known areas is the Shankill, from *sean chill* meaning 'old church'.

Placename (Druidic)	Irish form	Original meaning
Boheraphuca	bóthar an phúca	road of the Pooka
Loch Gillagancan	loch giolla gan ceann	lake of the man without a head
Sheetrim	sidh dhruim	fairy ridge

Placename (Christian)	Irish form	Original meaning
Croaghpatrick	cruach Phádraig	Patrick's hill
Donaghmore	domhnach mór	big church/Sunday
Monasteranenagh	mainstear an aonaigh	monastery of the fair

We have increasingly good written records of Ireland's history and literature from about the seventh century and many of these preserve oral traditions that were much older. The writing was in both Latin and Irish, languages that continued to flourish, in spite of the Viking raids that started around AD 795 and continued until 1014, when the Danes were finally defeated by Brian Boru at the battle of Clontarf. When we reel history off in terms of dates and key figures, we provide a very superficial, and therefore distorted, account of the times.

The Vikings

Many of the Vikings came as raiders and left after they had pillaged and plundered, but many others settled in Ireland, at first speaking their Scandinavian dialects but gradually learning Irish and adding some Viking words to their newly acquired tongue. We can recognise their linguistic contributions in such words as *bróg*, which comes from Old Norse *brók*, 'leg covering'. The Vikings gave the same word to the English, who turned it into 'breeches' or 'britches'. It is perhaps worth considering why the English and the Irish borrowed the same word and treated it so differently, in terms of its sound and its meaning.

One is tempted to believe that the American linguist, Benjamin Whorf, was correct in suggesting that the speakers of each language

> **Benjamin Whorf (1897–1941) claimed that a group's language had a profound effect on their behaviour and view of the world.**
>
> *We dissect nature along the lines laid down by our native languages.*
>
> **His ideas, collected in *Language, Thought and Reality* (ed. John B. Carroll, 1965) have influenced generations of scholars and are reflected in Brian Friel's play, *Translations*.**

have a unique way of looking at the universe and of constructing their view of reality.

We can leave the realm of speculation, however, when we point to the influence of the Vikings on the map. They first raided *Lambay Island* near Dublin, a name that is tautological since *lamb* + *ey* means 'lamb island'. A similar use of Viking *ay* or *ey* can be found in *Dalkey* (Dublin) from Danish *dalk* + *ey*, 'thorn + island' and in Welsh *Swansea*, meaning 'swans island'. Other Viking settlements in Ireland are suggested by '-ford', from Old Norse *fjöthr*, 'narrow inlet of the sea', as in *Carlingford Lough*, *Longford*, *Waterford* and *Wexford*. Further relics of the Northmen's influence include *vig*, 'bay', as in *Wicklow* or Scottish *Wick*, and their partiality for good fishing is immortalised in *Leixlip* on the Liffey, a name that comes from *hlaxa* + *hlaup*, 'salmon's leap'.

The Vikings were finally defeated in Ireland in 1014, and during the next century and a half the Irish language and culture flourished. It was perhaps inevitable, however, that the Normans, who conquered England in 1066, would cast acquisitive eyes on Ireland. They did, and the long struggle between the countries, both territorial and linguistic, began just over a hundred years after the defeat of the Anglo-Saxons at the Battle of Hastings.

The Normans

There are fewer relics of the Norman invasion on the map than we might expect but they can be found, especially in the affix *buirgéis* meaning 'borough' in such names as *Borrisnafarney* (Tipperary) from *buirgéis* + *fearna*, 'borough of the alder trees'. Other influences from French can be seen in the use of *ville*, 'town', *point*, 'location', and *cour*, 'courtyard', in *Charleville* (Cork), *Jerpoint Abbey* (Kilkenny), and *Powerscourt* (Wicklow). Perhaps the relative insignificance of French influence on places should not surprise us when we remember that the Normans who came to Ireland did not come directly from France but from Wales and south-west England.

The effect on the map from the English language dates mainly from the colonisation, known as the 'plantations', that occurred under the Tudors and Stuarts. Some of the names, *Greencastle* (Antrim), *Jamestown* (Leitrim) or *Newcastle* (Tipperary), are English, while others such as *Portmarnock* (Dublin), *Portstewart* (Derry) and *Stewartstown* (Tyrone) are Scottish. Sometimes the anglicised place-names were associated with people such as *Mountjoy* (Tyrone); often they were direct translations as when *Carraig Dhubh* became *Black Rock*; and occasionally, as with *Londonderry*, they were blends. The London merchants who put venture capital into the north-east of Ireland were honoured by the renaming of the town that originally came from *doire*, 'oakgrove'. Such renaming has, on occasion, met with fierce opposition. Indeed, even in 1998, a walk through the city revealed two sets of slogans, one proclaiming:

It's Londonderry.

and another carrying the message:

You are now entering free Derry.

Our journey of discovery is about to begin as we explore when and how and why English became nativised in Ireland. It is worth reminding ourselves at the outset what everyone already knows. The language spoken in Ireland is similar to the language spoken in England – similar but by no means identical. At some level, most Irish people are aware that Green English is a grafted tongue, an English foliage on an Irish stem, still nourished by an Irish root. Occasionally, an English person recognises this truth. Peter Lennon, a journalist, wrote as follows in *The Guardian* (17 May 1984):

Bruce Arnold, an Englishman working in Ireland for many years as a political journalist, finally adapted 'with a mixture of hope and despair' to what he describes as Ireland's 'essential foreignness over which the English language throws a misleading cloak'.

Sometimes, the differences are thought to be merely those of accent. Yet, it goes much deeper than that. Whether in speech or in writing, the Irish use English with uninhibited vigour. John Braidwood, a Scot who lectured for many years in Belfast, was on the right track when he claimed, as long ago as 1964:

> *If ever an age had the gift of the gab, that age was the Elizabethan. If ever a nation had the gift of the gab, that nation is the Irish. It is not suggested for a moment that the Irish inherited the gift from the Elizabethans, for the Irish gift is of ancient origin ... But in both cases, Elizabethan and Irish, the gift is one of imagination too ... In particular, a long period of bilingualism, during which English was assimilated to Irish speech habits, became a thing apart ...*

> (*Ulster Dialects*, 1964: 81)

Our journey will explore the linguistic creation that Braidwood recognised as 'a thing apart'. The route will take us through Ireland, and beyond, because traces of it are to be found in America and Australia, in Africa and Asia, and in all the parts of the world where the Irish have gone as missionaries or teachers, soldiers or settlers. In 1590, while English and Scots were being encouraged to settle in Ireland, Samuel Daniels wondered:

> *And who in time knows whither we may vent*
> *The treasures of our tongue, to what strange shores*
> *This gain of our best glory shall be sent*
> *T'enrich unknowing nations with our stores?*
> *What worlds in th'yet unformed occident*
> *May come refin'd with th'accents that are ours?*
> *Or who can tell for what great work in hand*
> *The greatness of our style is now ordain'd?*

He could not have guessed how often the 'treasures' of the English tongue were to be carried in Irish mouths.

CHAPTER TWO

'In the beginning was the focal...'

The history of a language is often a story of possession and dispossession, territorial struggle and the establishment or imposition of a culture.

(Tom Paulin, *A New Look at the Language Question*, 1983: 1)

Most Irish people know the story of King Brian Boru. On 23 April 1014, the eighty-seven-year-old King of Munster won the Battle of Clontarf, defeating King Mael Morda of Leinster and his Viking allies. Brian himself was partly Scandinavian and he is an early example of the settlers who came to Ireland and became 'more Irish than the Irish themselves'. But there is another story from the early part of the second millennium that has been told many times and with varying degrees of elaboration. Douglas Hyde quotes it as follows:

By him (Brian Boru were erected also noble churches and sanctuaries in Erin .... many works also, and repairs were made by him .... By him were made bridges and causeways and high roads. By him were strengthened also the dúns and fortresses and islands and celebrated royal forts of Munster .... The peace of Erin was proclaimed by him, both of churches and people so that peace throughout all Erin was made in his time .... After the banishment of the foreigners out of all Erin and after Erin was reduced to a state of peace, a single woman came from Torach in the north of Erin to Clíodhna in the south of Erin, carrying a ring of gold on a horse-rod, and she was neither robbed nor insulted.

(D. Hyde, *A Literary History of Ireland*, 1967: 443–4)

Thomas Moore tells the same story in words and music in 'Rich and Rare':

> *Rich and rare were the gems she wore,*
> *And a bright gold ring on her wand she bore;*
> *But oh! her beauty was far beyond*
> *Her sparking gems, or snow-white wand.*
>
> *'Lady! dost thou not fear to stray,*
> *So lone and lovely through this bleak way?*
> *Are Erin's sons so good or so cold,*
> *As not to be tempted by woman or gold?'*
>
> *'Sir Knight! I feel not the least alarm,*
> *No son of Erin will offer me harm:-*
> *For though they love woman and golden store,*
> *Sir Knight! they love honour and virtue more!'*
>
> *On she went, and her maiden smile*
> *In safety lighted her round the Green Isle;*
> *And blest for ever is she who relied*
> *Upon Erin's honour and Erin's pride.*

This is an intriguing story but, like many stories of the period, one for which we have very little background information. We do not know how such a woman acquired her wealth, or why she felt the need to prove that she could travel anywhere in safety, even without an escort. One thing we do know, however, is that she would almost certainly have spoken a form of Irish Gaelic, and perhaps also Latin. She may have understood the Germanic dialects spoken by Danes and Norwegians. It is unlikely that she knew English, unless it happened that her family was involved in trading with the Angles or Saxons. Trade, like love, finds a linguistic way.

The English in Ireland

We cannot, with any certainty, trace English in Ireland back earlier than the twelfth century, although it is likely that English-speaking traders had visited Ireland for centuries before that. If only we could uncover linguistic DNA or subject samples of language to carbon dating, then researchers would be able to say who spoke what to whom. Unfortunately, speech leaves no fossil traces.

Within a hundred years of the Norman Conquest of England (1066), speakers of English began to appear in Ireland and the documented history of contact between the islands began. These first English-speaking settlers were not aggressive conquerors, as they are sometimes simplistically perceived. The history of contact between England and Ireland is much more complex than that. First, there was an apparent religious reason for the invasions. In 1155, Pope Adrian IV (the one and only English Pope, Nicholas Breakspeare) gave Ireland to King Henry II of England so that he could implement religious reforms there. Henry II (1133–89) (who is best known, perhaps, for having instigated the murder of Thomas à Becket in Canterbury Cathedral on 29 December 1170) was almost certainly inspired less by religious zeal than by a desire to augment his kingdom, when he eventually set out for Ireland in 1171.

The second reason for the influx of English speakers was infighting in Ireland. When Diarmaid was ousted from his Leinster kingdom in 1168, he asked Henry II for permission to raise an army from among Henry's subjects in order to fight for the return of his kingdom. Diarmaid won the help of the Norman Strongbow (otherwise known as Richard Fitzgilbert, Earl of Pembroke) and two thousand of his men, by promising his daughter, Aoife, in marriage, and the kingdom of Leinster on his death. Diarmaid's plan worked. Strongbow and his followers landed in Wexford in May 1169 and helped Diarmaid to regain his kingdom. Diarmaid's pleasure in winning back his birthright was short-lived. By 1171 he was dead and Strongbow was King of Leinster.

Henry II sailed to Ireland in the same year. The plan was to ensure that Strongbow did not become too powerful and to avoid criticism from the new pope, Alexander III, over the murder of Thomas à Becket. By 1172, Henry had received homage from Strongbow and a number of Irish princes. And thereafter, the Norman conquest of Ireland was swift, efficient and comprehensive. The Treaty of Windsor suggests that by 1175 as much as half of Ireland was under Norman rule. By 1250, three-quarters of the country had been divided into shires with English, of some sort, spoken in all of the major settlements.

Relics of Yola English

The first Norman lords to settle in Ireland almost certainly spoke Norman French and may have used Latin to communicate with the

The Spread of English in the Thirteenth Century

Irish. However, the two thousand soldiers would probably have spoken Welsh, Welsh English and the dialect of south-west England. There are no records of their speech. We can gain some idea of what it was like by looking at a brief sample from a poem probably written in Kildare around 1300, roughly the time William Wallace (?1272–1305) was fighting for Scottish freedom. Apart from unfamiliar spelling and the letter 'þ', representing modern 'th', the language and the sentiments are surprisingly modern:

þis world is loue is gon awai,	This world's love is gone away
So dew on grasse in somer is dai,	Like dew on grass on a summer's day
Few þer beþ, weilawai,	Few there be, alas
þat louiþ goddis lore ...	That love God's wisdom ...

and in the verse that complains about the way the weak have their lands taken by the strong:

And þos hoblurs namelich	And those soldiers namely
þat husbond benimeþ eri of grund,	That deprive farmers of their ground,
Men ne schold ham biri in non chirch,	No one should bury them in church
Bot cast ham ute as a hund.	But cast them out as one might a dog.

The English used in such verse is as standard as any written in England of the period and tells us little about pronunciation. It seems likely, however, that the English speakers used 'f' for 'wh' in words such as 'what'; 'v' for 'f' in words such as 'for'; and 'z' not 's' in words like 'summer' – just as some people still do in parts of Somerset and Devon even today. The reason for such an assumption is simple: these features occurred in representations of spoken English in Ireland from the fourteenth century and continued to be found in the dialects of English from the Fingal area near Dublin and from Forth, the eastern-most tip of Wexford, until the nineteenth century:

Fade teil thee zo lournach, co Joane, zo knaggee?
Th'weithest all curcagh, wafur, an cornee.
Lidge w'ouse an a milagh, 'tis gaay an louthee

Huck nigher, y'art scuddeen, fartoo zo hachee?
(What ails thee so melancholy, quoth John, so crabby?
You seem all snappy, uneasy, and fretful.
Lie with us on a (bank of) clover, it's lovely and shaded.
Come closer, you are shaking, why are you so angry?)

(J.J. Hogan, The English Language in Ireland, 1927: 94)

This type of dialect was known as 'Yola', meaning 'old', and it preserved some features of Old English that have been lost from today's standard language. It is also easy to find examples of English written to represent Irish speech, where 'th', as in 'thank' and 'they', are written as 't' in 'tanked' and 'd' in 'dey'. The Irish playwright George Farquhar (1678–1707) gives the Irish servant, Teague, the forms *dere* for 'there' and *fet* for 'faith' as well as *fat* for 'what' and *Carick-Vergus* for Carrickfergus in his play *Twin Rivals* (1702). It is highly probable, however, that many of the English also used such pronunciations at an earlier time, if we judge by the early spelling of 'Catholic' as 'Cat(t)olic' or by the diminutive forms of popular names. The English used and still use 'Tony' as a short form of 'Anthony' and 'Bet' or 'Betty' as an abbreviation of 'Elizabeth'.

By the end of the thirteenth century, Yola seems to have been used in the east, at least as far north as Tyrone and Armagh, along the east coast to the south of Wexford, and in all urbanised areas as far west as Galway. Of course, this did not mean that everyone in the anglicised areas spoke English. The lords and leaseholders were mostly English in origin and so would have had English as their mother tongue. However, the labouring classes were almost exclusively Irish and would have continued to be Irish speaking, although some of them, at least, would have learnt as much English as they needed to cook, clean or attend to the children in the manors, or to negotiate conditions for farm work. It has normally been the role of the socially or economically weak to learn the language of the powerful.

The revival of Irish

A hundred years later, however, the English language was in retreat. The Norman gentry had adopted Irish customs, Irish dress, Irish names and the Irish language. They had become hibernicised. Some of the English yeomen had also intermarried with the Irish and become indistinguishable from them, while others had abandoned the Irish countryside for the security of the Pale, the area around Dublin. This word comes from Norman French *pal*, meaning 'stake, pole', and was first used in Ireland to refer to a section of land enclosed by pales or wooden strips. It is from this period that the phrase 'beyond the pale' came to mean 'outside the limits of security or social convention'.

By 1366, the government in London was so worried by the perilous state of the English language in Ireland that it passed the Statutes of Kilkenny. These are interesting, not only linguistically but also socially, in that they seem to assume that the native Irish were enemies of England, rather than subjects. The legislation was an attempt to put a finger in the linguistic dyke and to preserve the eastern part of the country for English laws, English people and the English language. It is strange, then, that it used a form of French to insist that English people should *prendre et user la lang Engleis* (adopt and use the English language), that all clerics (whether English, Irish or Norman) should speak English, even if that meant giving them *respit de la lang Engleis apprendre* (some extra time to learn the English language). Even Gaelic games were banned, especially *des Jues que homme appelle horlinge* (the games that people call hurling). By 1430, Archbishop John Swayne of Armagh wrote that:

... the housbonde pepill for the meschefe and governances aforesaide be gone out of the londe ... into englonde [so that] *there is more gone oute of the londe of the kyngis lege pepyll than be in it.*	... the farming people because of the troubles and previously described systems of government have left the land ... for England so that more of the king's liegemen have left the land than have stayed on it.

So far, we have looked at the first wave of Germanic dialects to wash over Ireland. The Vikings first struck Ireland in 795. Over the next two hundred and fifty years, they established settlements, but by 1050 they had either been absorbed by the Irish or had moved away. A century later, the Normans with their English-speaking followers moved into Ireland and spread their influence and a form of English into all but the remotest areas of the island. Yet, by 1400 they too had either been largely assimilated or had returned to England, and the Irish language was once again dominant.

The hibernicisation of incomers has been noted many times. It was such a feature of immigrants to Ireland that the truism was coined about visitors becoming 'more Irish than the Irish themselves'. What is less frequently mentioned is that the linguistic influences were not all one way. In spite of the claims by generations of writers on the history of the English language that 'outside of place-names ... the influence of Celtic upon the English language is almost negligible' (Baugh, 1959: 85) or that the Celtic languages gave no more than 'a dozen words to English' (Wakelin, 1972: 126), it will be evident from subsequent chapters that the Celtic language gave much more to English than has ever been acknowledged.

> *One thing is clear: the Celtic languages of Roman Britain had hardly any influence on the language spoken by the Anglo-Saxons. Only a handful of Celtic words came into English at the time – such as* crag, combe, bin, cross, brock *(badger), and* tor *(peak).*
>
> (David Crystal, *The English Language*, 1988: 153)

The origin of 'she'

But let us, for the moment, consider just one word here, the word 'she'. No linguist has been able to offer a satisfactory explanation for the existence of the pronoun 'she' in English. In Old English, the personal pronouns were more complex than they are today and four cases were distinguished, namely, nominative, accusative, dative and genitive.

FIRST PERSON

Case	Singular	Dual	Plural
Nominative	ic = I	wit = we two	we = we
Accusative	me (mec) = me	unc = us two	us (usic) = us
Dative	me = to me	unc = to us two	us = to us
Genitive	min = mine	uncer = our (two)	use (ure) = our

SECOND PERSON

Case	Singular	Dual	Plural
Nominative	ðu = thou	ʒit = you two	ʒe = you/ye
Accusative	ðe = thee	(ʒ)inc = you two	eow = you
Dative	ðe (ðec) = to you	(ʒ)inc = to you two	eow = to you
Genitive	ðin = thine	(ʒ)incer = your (two)	eower = your

THIRD PERSON

Case	Male	Female	Neuter	Plural
Nominative	he = he	he(o) = she	hit = it	hie = they
Accusative	hine = him	hie = her	hit = it	hie = they
Dative	him = to him	hi(e)re = to her	him = to it	him = to them
Genitive	his = his	hi(e)re = her	his = its	hiera = their

Even without training, a modern reader can recognise the ancestors of modern 'I' (and compare it to German *ich*), 'me', 'mine', 'thou', 'thee', 'thine', 'you' and 'your' (especially when we remember that 'ð' and 'ʒ' were pronounced like modern 'th' and 'y'). We can also see where modern 'it', 'he' and 'him' come from. The two pronouns that differ quite markedly from Modern English are the forms for 'she' and for 'they', 'them' and 'their'. In fact, in the tenth century, there were parts of England where the same pronoun *he* could mean 'he', 'she' and 'they'. Such a high degree of ambiguity was not allowed to continue. Speakers, especially in the north of England, began to adopt the Norse forms *þai*, *þeʒʒm* and *þeʒʒre*, which developed into modern 'they', 'them' and 'their'. The change from *he(o)* to 'she' is much less easy to account for. No dialect of English or Norse had a personal pronoun that would or could have developed directly into 'she', although many etymologists have struggled to explain it by invoking combinations of Old English and Old Norse personal pronouns and by suggesting that the demonstrative pronoun *seo*, probably pronounced like 'say + o', can help in explaining the shift from 'he' to 'she'. Indeed, the *Oxford English Dictionary* takes approximately one quarter the length of this book to discuss the various possibilities. However, one source that is not considered is the Irish third person feminine pronoun *sí*, a form that is and was pronounced like modern 'she', and which can be traced back to Old Celtic *sí*, meaning 'she'. Irish clerics and scribes were to be found in many communities in England and we do not even have to discount the fact that the Scandinavians were partly responsible for the dissemination of 'she' because:

> ... *the early Scandinavian settlements (ninth century and earlier) in this country were mainly Danish and were on the Eastern side of England. Norwegian settlements occurring somewhat later (mainly in the first half of the tenth century by men **who had been living in Ireland**) were in the northwestern counties and the North and West Ridings of Yorkshire.*

(M. Wakelin, *English Dialects: An Introduction*, 1972: 18, bold mine)

Word origins?

The suggestion about the Gaelic origin of 'she' is perhaps controversial, but this fact is notable in itself. Why has there been such a long-standing reluctance to recognise the presence of Celtic words in the English language? Many writers have acknowledged the existence of a 'few' Celtic words, but, interestingly, the individual words in that 'few' tend to vary from scholar to scholar. And what is invariably underplayed is the phenomenon known as 'multiple etymologies', where a similar form occurs in more than one of the languages in contact and enhances the likelihood of its selection by all the speakers. If we take the dialect word *keek*, 'peep', for example, the *Collins English Dictionary* suggests that it possibly comes from Dutch *kiken*, 'to look'. But Irish Gaelic also has *caoch*, meaning 'peep' as in the children's action rhyme:

Buail ar an doras		Beat on the door	
Caoch isteach		Peep in	
Tóg an laiste		Lift the latch	
Siubhal isteach.		Walk in.	

What is possible is that a form like *keek* occurred in the Anglo-Saxon dialects and in the Celtic languages and in Dutch. The table below offers a very small sample of words that have parallels in both English and Irish. Similar chance likenesses must also have occurred when the Anglo-Saxons first settled among Celtic speakers.

English Word	Meaning	Irish Word	Meaning
ark	ark, chest	arc	meal chest
bat	club for hitting ball	bata	stick
buck	male goat	boc	male goat
bumble bee		bumbóg	bee
cleg	horsefly	cuileóg	fly
crag	rock	carraig	rock
cuckoo		cuach	cuckoo
dark		dorcha	dark
gammy	lame	(cos) cham	lame (leg)
market		margadh	market
take		tóg	take

The tenth word in our list, *market*, reminds us that linguistic origins may not be clear cut. Old English *market* probably comes from Old Norman French *market*, although it could also derive from Latin *mercatus*. Modern French *marché* seems to derive from a Central form of Old French *marchiet, marchié*. Irish Gaelic may have borrowed its word *margadh* from the Viking forms *markaðr, marknaðr* but the Vikings had, in their turn, borrowed it either from the French or from Latin. We must remember that scribes and poets of the period rarely concentrated on such mundane activities as markets. And *take* is certainly Old English but it replaced *niman*, possibly under the influence of Celtic forms, whereas German retained *nehmen*.

Early Irish English

We can leave controversy, temporarily, to illustrate some of the characteristics of early Irish English. We can do this simply by examining a Dedication to *Secreta Secretorum*, a book of instruction for noblemen, written by James Young about 1422:

> *In the Honoure of the Hey Trynyte, Fadyr, Sone, and Holy gooste, Almyghti god; oure lady Seynte Mary, and al the holy hollowes of hewyn: To yow, nobyll and gracious lorde, Iamys de Botillere, Erle of Ormonde, lieutenaunt of oure lege lorde, kynge henry the fyfte in Irland, humbly recommendyth hime youre pouer Seruant, Iames yonge, to youre hey lordshipp: altymes desyringe in chryste, yowre honoure and profite of body and Sowle, and wyth al myn herte the trynyte afor-sayde besechynge that he hit ever Encrese.*

The paragraph is at least as easy to read as Chaucer's *Canterbury Tales* and is reasonably typical of written English of the period. The first thing a modern reader notices is the inconsistency of the spelling, which did not begin to be standardised until after William Caxton had set up England's first printing press in England in 1477. 'James' occurs as both *Iamys* and *Iames*; 'your' as *youre* and *yowre*. Capitalisation is also random. The word for 'Trinity' occurs as both *Trynyte* and *trynyte*, *body* is written with a lower-case 'b' whereas *Sowle* is capitalised, as is *Seynte*, 'Saint', whereas 'Mary', 'Henry', 'Young' and 'Christ' are all written with lower case initial letters. All the words used can be found in Modern English with the exception of *hollowes*, meaning 'saints', although we still talk about *Hallowe'en*, meaning 'the evening before All Saints Day'. The sentence structure of the passage is more balanced and the sentiments more fulsome than modern styles might dictate, but there are only two positions where we cannot give a word for word modern equivalent and these occur in the opening and closing phrases, where we would say 'To the honour of the High Trinity' and 'that he always increases it'.

The prose in English of the fourteenth and fifteenth centuries was probably written by people of Norman or English ancestry who were eager for advancement within the English-oriented establishment. The same point is likely to hold true for the poetry that flourished in the monastic settlements of Kildare. The Statutes of Kilkenny forbade any *merus hibernicus*, 'mere Irishman', to join a religious order in the areas of Ireland under English jurisdiction. This rule may not, of course, have been applied rigorously or it may not have included women. What we can say is that poetry of all types flourished in the Kildare monastic settlements, probably prior to 1315. We find verse that concentrates on the transitoriness of life and natural beauty:

þis world is loue is gon awai	The world's love has gone away
So dew on grasse in somer is dai	Like dew on grass on a summer's day

(J.J. Hogan, *The English Language in Ireland*, 1927: 17)

The language here is readily understood by any English speaker today, and it is only fair to acknowledge that this theme is found in literatures in every part of the world and may even be encapsulated by a Latin dictum:

Sic transit gloria mundi.	Thus passes the glory of the world.

The theme may, however, have been reinforced by Irish traditions. It is certainly found in Gaelic literature, as in the following poem, for example, which is hundreds of years older than the Kildare couplet:

Ind ráith I comair in dairfedo	The fort beside the oakgrove
ba Bruidgi, ba Cathail	was Bruidge's, was Cathal's
ba Aedo, ba Ailello	was Aedh's, was Ailill's
ba Conaing, ba Cuilíní	was Conaing's, was Cuilíne's
ocus ba Máele Dúin.	And it was Mael Dun's
Int ráith d'éis cach ríg ar uair	One by one the kings sleep in the earth
ocus int slúaig, foait in-úir.	and the fort still endures.

(J. Carney, *Medieval Irish Lyrics*, 1985: x-xi)

We also find sharp wit and high-spirited fantasy in 'The Land of Cockaygne'. This poem satirises the supposed immorality of the monks and nuns at the Cistercian Abbey of Inishloughnacht – a name that means 'island of sweet milk' and that is reminiscent of both the Garden of Eden and the biblical land flowing with milk and honey:

'THE LAND OF COCKAYGNE'	GENESIS 2, 10–12
Of the streams all the mould Stones precious and gold There is saphire and uniune, Carbuncle and astiune, Smaragde, lugre, and prassiune, Beryl, onyx and topiasune, Amethyst and chrysolite, Chalcedony and epitite.	And a river went out of Eden to water the garden; and from thence it was parted, and became into four heads. The name of the first is Pison; that is it which compasseth the whole land of Havilah, where there is gold … there is bdellium and the onyx stone …

Again, the theme is not quintessentially Irish. However, the interest in colours and jewels can find parallels in the eighth-century *Immram Curaig Máile Dúine* (The Voyage of Mael Dún's Coracle), especially the visit to the ninth island, where Mael Dún and his followers find a huge treasure of gold and jewels, guarded by a cat.

Undervalued writings

There is no doubt that the English language written in Ireland is and was similar to the language written in England. We can recognise it as being essentially the same medium that was used by Geoffrey Chaucer (?1340–1400). He produced narrative, satiric, and elegiac verse of a very high order and was, incidentally, page to the Countess of Ulster, the daughter-in-law of Edward III. More of his work has survived than that of any of his contemporaries, whether in England or in Ireland. However, that was a matter of chance and Chaucer himself expresses the fear that his writings will suffer from being transcribed incorrectly:

And for ther is so gret diversite	And because there is such great diversity

In Englissh and in writyng of oure tonge,	In English and in the writing of our tongue,
So preye I God that non myswrite the,	I pray to God that nobody writes thee incorrectly,
Ne mysmetre for defaute of tonge.	Or uses incorrect metres because of weaknesses of language.

(*Troilus and Criseyde*, V, 1793–96)

The value of the medieval literature written in English in Ireland, whether drama, prose or poetry, has been consistently underrated. A brief examination of the Middle English syllabuses of university undergraduate courses in England shows that the considerable body of Kildare poems remains largely unstudied, unlisted and unappreciated. This is a strange state of affairs when contrasted with the time devoted to 'Sir Gawain and the Green Knight'. This is a beautiful poem but in a dialect that is no longer accessible to speakers of Modern English, as is clear from the following couplet:

þrete is vnþryuande in þede þer I lende,	Threatening is valueless where I come from,
And vche gift þat is geven not with goud wylle.	And so is every gift that is not given with good wishes.

(1499–1500)

By the late fifteenth century, the English language was less vigorous in Ireland than it had been for almost three hundred years. It was a minority language, used widely only by recent immigrants, by English officials in the Dublin area and by the settlers in the baronies of Forth and Bargy in Wexford. Stanihurst wrote his *Description of Irelande* in 1577, almost a century later than the period described here, but he stressed the loyalty of Wexford people to the English language:

But of all other places, Weiseforde with the territorye bayed, and perclosed within the riuer called the Pill, was so quite estranged from Irishry, as if a traualler of the Irish (which was rare in those dayes) had

picht his foote within the pile and spoken Irishe, the Weisfordians would
commaunde hym forthwith to turne the other end of his tongue, and
speake Englishe ...

English would probably have disappeared as completely from Ireland
by the end of the sixteenth century as the Scandinavian dialects had,
if the country had not experienced a second wave of English, starting
in the reign of Mary Tudor (1553–58), and becoming a flood in the
reigns of Elizabeth (1558–1603) and James I (1603–25).

There is a well-known anonymous verse in the language of the
fourteenth century:

Icham of Irlaunde
and of the holy londe
of irlande
gode sire pray ich þe
for of saynte charite
come ant daunce wyt me
in irlaunde.

This is a pleasant, apparently unpretentious lyric that does not
appear to deal with anything very profound. However, its theme was
to resonate throughout the following centuries. This was perhaps the
beginning of the large-scale emigration from Ireland. Irish people settled in all parts of the world, from Bantry Bay in Cork to Bantry Bay in
Cape Town, from Dungannon in Tyrone to Dungannon in Canada,
from the island of Ireland in the northern hemisphere to the tropical
island of New Ireland in the South Pacific.

Like a lot of medieval writing, however, *Icham of Irlaunde* may not be as simple and unpretentious as it appears. In the first place, the word 'dance' is of uncertain origin although it now occurs as *danse* in French, *damhsa* in Irish, *dança* in Portuguese, *danza* in Italian and *Tanz* in German. The word *may* be Romance in origin, although it does not derive from Latin. It *may* be from Old High German *dansôn*, 'to draw, stretch out' although that meaning is not altogether satisfactory. What is of interest to us is that the occurrence of 'dance' in this poem is one of the earliest in the English language, and because of that its meaning is not absolutely certain. It is possible that it has religious overtones. After all, in early translations of the Second Book of Samuel, King David worships God before the Ark of the Covenant by dancing, *And David danced before the Lord with all his might* ... (6: 14). And Psalm 149 exhorts the people of Israel: *Let them praise his name in the dance.*

It is also uncertain whether the speaker is male or female, living or dead. We should also remember that the theme of the *danse macabre* was popular in medieval art and literature and in this dance of death, people are led to their graves by the personification of death.

Green English

CHAPTER THREE

Planter English

*How Irish people use the English language does more than reveal class,
as it might do in England; it can also give away tribal loyalties.*

(Heather Elliott, *Contemporary Women Writers
in the North of Ireland*, 1988: 49)

Just as the Vikings were becoming hibernicised, the Normans
invaded England and soon claimed Ireland as part of their extended
kingdom. By 1250, three-quarters of Ireland had been divided into
shires and English was used in all the large settlements. However, the
Anglo-Normans, like the Vikings before them, gradually adopted
Irish traditions and the Irish language The Fitzgeralds became the
MacGearailts, the Bryons became the O'Briens and the hibernicisation was almost complete. By the early years of the sixteenth century,
Irish Gaelic had regained sway in Ireland. The linguistic preference
for Irish had been helped by the Reformation, which took root in
England but not in Ireland.

In this chapter and the next, we shall explore the separate linguistic strands that were woven together in Ireland. We will examine
both English and Scottish varieties of Planter English and the
Hiberno-English that they helped to create. This type of description,
where different linguistic aspects are treated individually, is akin to
describing the human body in terms of legs, trunk, arms and head. It
is the truth but it is not the whole truth. It may also suggest that these
three Englishes are distinct and separable. They are not. It is easy, of
course, to pick out words such as *áfoot*, *bairn* and *banshee* and to relate
them unequivocally to English, Scots and Irish Gaelic respectively.
But Green English is more than the sum of its parts in the same way

that a person is more than just a collection of bones and tissues. The English verb *destroy*, for example, still means 'ruin, spoil, render useless' but, in Ireland, it took on the meanings of *mill*, its equivalent in Irish, and could thus also imply 'suffer from', as in:

I'm destroyed with the cold this last fortnight.

The Scottish adjective *wee*, meaning 'small', has absorbed some of the meaning of Irish *beag* in that it can mean 'young' as well as 'small':

Their wee girl is as big as the father now.

and Irish Gaelic also influenced the meaning of 'young' in the shopkeeper's claim that the facecloth he was selling was 'as big as a young towel'. A good analogy is that the three types of English are like flour, water and eggs. Before we allow them to interact in cooking, their differences are clear, but after cooking, they have combined to create something new and indivisible.

A further clarification should be made. All varieties of English in Ireland – and elsewhere – are influenced by education and media norms. Many words or phrases that were widespread fifty years ago are now found only in rural areas or in the speech of older people. Young urban dwellers in Belfast, Cork or Dublin can still be differentiated by their accents but their usage increasingly resembles that of their age group in Edinburgh, New York or Sydney. Many young people continue to have a passive knowledge of the patterns described in the following pages but the homogenisation of world English has not passed Ireland by.

A graphic illustration of this point was made by a middle-aged woman I once interviewed. We were talking about words changing and she said: *They were always 'saibies' in my day; then a body took to calling them 'scallions'; we'll be calling them 'spring onions' next.* Recently, I visited the town where I made the recording and saw the sign 'SPRING ONIONS' in the greengrocer's.

Rupture with Rome

It is often suggested that the Reformation began on 3 October 1517. On that day, a thirty-four-year-old Augustinian monk nailed ninety-five points to the door of Wittenberg Cathedral, challenging certain aspects of the authority of the Roman Church. Martin Luther, however, was only one in a long line of critics and he, like those before him, was not at first thinking of breaking with Rome. The writer of 'The Land of Cockaygne' pre-empted, by over two hundred years, many of the Reformers' criticisms of scandalous behaviour. Geoffrey Chaucer, in his day, had also criticised the Church in his depiction of the Friar, the Monk and the Summoner and had praised the *povre persoun*, 'poor priest', pointing out:

> *And shame it is, if a preest take keep*
> *A shiten shepherde and a clene sheep.*

Even in England, there was no real stomach among most people for the Reformation. Like so many important occurrences in history, it nearly didn't happen. Henry VII (1485–1509) was renowned for his carefulness with money. (One wonders how the history of the world might have changed if Christopher Columbus, on his visit to England in 1485, had been successful in raising money for his 'new route to the Indies'.) Such 'carefulness' with money was more important to Henry than religious zeal. In 1501, he declined the Pope's invitation to lead a Crusade against the Ottoman Empire. Thrift also played a role in his marrying off Catherine of Aragon to his second son, Henry, when his first son, Arthur, died. He did not want to return the dowry that Catherine had brought to England.

Catherine of Aragon was a devout Catholic and, at first, so was Henry VIII. Pope Leo X rewarded him with the title *Fidei Defensor*, 'Defender of the Faith', for his treatise defending the validity of the seven sacraments. By 1530, Henry VIII wanted to divorce Catherine and marry Anne Boleyn. In different circumstances, his request for a divorce might have been granted. He had, after all, married his brother's widow and there were royal precedents for annulments. In

1499, for example, Louis XII had divorced his wife, Jeanne, and married Anne of Brittany. But Pope Clement VII was unwilling to antagonise Catherine's uncle, King Charles V of Spain and ruler of what was left of the Holy Roman Empire. Consequently, in 1534, Henry VIII broke with Rome and declared himself the head of the Church in England.

At first, Henry's rupture with Rome made little difference in Ireland. Kings had quarrelled with the Church before and the rift had been healed in the next reign. When Henry died in 1547, he was succeeded by Edward VI, who was a devout Protestant. Many acts were passed enshrining Protestantism in the law, but it was clear that he was unlikely to survive childhood. Edward died in 1553 and Catherine of Aragon's fiercely Catholic daughter, Mary Tudor, became Queen of England. Her arrival on the throne may initially have pleased the inhabitants of Ireland, both English and Irish. However, Mary began the large-scale plantations of Ireland that were to usher in almost four centuries of violent struggle. Her reasons were twofold. She wanted to strengthen and extend her power; and the population of London is thought to have reached 200,000, so there were English people to spare. When she was succeeded by her twenty-five-year-old sister, Elizabeth, in 1558, the movement away from Rome began again and in 1570 Elizabeth was excommunicated by Pope Pius V.

Yola

The Old English, who had stayed in Ireland, began to find that they had more in common with the Catholic native Irish than with their Protestant contemporaries in England. From the middle of the sixteenth century, we find increasingly frequent comments on the unEnglishness of the Old English in Ireland, in both behaviour and language. In 1577, Stanihurst tells the story of an English peer who visited Ireland for the first time and decided that he would have little difficulty in learning Irish:

> *... supposing that the blunt people had pratled Irishe, all the while they iangled Englishe. Howbeit to this day, the dregs of the olde auncient Chaucer English, are kept ...*

By 1578, the Lord Chancellor of England criticised the first settlers because:

> *... all [of them], and the most part with delight, even in Dublin, speak Irish, and greatly are spotted in manners, habit and conditions with Irish stains.*

In 1581, Sir Henry Wallop claimed:

> *... to this day they generally speake oulde English ...*

and Sir John Davies in A *Discovery of the State of Ireland*, published in 1613, went even further and said:

> *... the English, both Lords and Free-holders, became degenerate and meer Irish in their Language, in their apparrell, in their armes and manner of fight ... They did not only forget the English Language and scorne the use thereof, but grew to bee ashamed of their very English Names, though they were noble and of great Antiquity; and tooke Irish Surnames and Nicknames.*

The poet, Edmund Spenser, who wrote much of his *Faerie Queene* in Ireland, and who acquired Kilcolman Castle in Cork while he was Lord Deputy, distinguished between the 'Old' and the 'New' English and commented on the hibernicisation of the former in *View of the Present State of Ireland* (1596: 637):

> *Other greate howses there be of the old English in Ireland, which ... are nowe growen as Irish as O-hanlan's breeche.*

Thus, by the end of the sixteenth century, the Irish had coped with a religious conversion in the fifth century, with political incursions by Scandinavians in the ninth century and by Anglo-Normans in the twelfth, and they had, slowly but surely, assimilated the invaders. Just as the Irish people had absorbed the invaders, the Irish language had absorbed vocabulary from Latin, Norse and the Anglo-Normans.

From Latin *pax*, 'peace', they created *póg*, the Irish Gaelic word for 'kiss'; from the Vikings, they borrowed *scilling*, the word that is the equivalent of English 'shilling'; and from the Anglo-Normans, they adopted words such as *gúna*, from *goune*, 'gown, garment'.

> **The English word *gown* and its Irish equivalent *gúna* are both said to come from Old French *goune*. However, the Old French word came from Late Latin *gunna*, which is of Celtic origin, and is thought to refer to a garment made of leather or fur. Such facts suggest that the final word on Celtic influences has yet to be written.**

Separate development

The social conditions – where outsiders were absorbed – were not allowed to continue, however. Successive English governments, from Mary Tudor on, were determined to subdue the Irish and to bring the subjugation about by means of a massive resettlement programme. This was the second wave of English influence. And, since Ulster was the most troublesome province in terms of insurrections against the English, it was singled out for special treatment. The so-called 'Plantation of Ulster' was designed to turn this rebellious province into a stronghold of English law and authority. Prior to 1600, we have no reliable figures for settlement but the following estimates for 1611 are regarded as reasonably accurate.

County	Irish	Planters	Total
Antrim	8,965	7,074	16,039
Armagh	4,355	2,393	6,748
Cavan	8,218	6,485	14,703
Derry	5,306	4,428	9,734
Donegal	8,589	3,412	12,001
Down	8,643	6,540	15,183
Fermanagh	5,302	1,800	7,102
Monaghan	3,649	434	4,083
Tyrone	10,245	8,085	18,330
Total for Ulster	63,272	40,651	103,923

The ratio of three Irish to two Planters is probably accurate, although the numbers as a whole may be an underestimate. Additional waves of English speakers were encouraged from Scotland and England during the English Civil War between Cavaliers and Roundheads (1642–48) and again after the struggle between William of Orange and James II (1688–90). Estimates suggest that by 1733 the 38,459 Irish families in Ulster were outnumbered by the 62,624 Planter families.

The Planters in the south and east of Ireland were mainly English. This accounts, in part, for the difference of accent between speakers in Ulster and in the other three provinces. The difference was apparent even in the eighteenth century if we are to judge from a notice in the 'Pennsylvania Gazette' of 1771:

> *Ran away, Isaac Baxter ... a little pock-marked, and by his dialect may be known to be a native of the north of Ireland.*

It is true, of course, that the vast majority of speakers on the island remained Gaelic-speaking until the middle of the nineteenth century. By the beginning of the twentieth, however, everything was 'changed, changed utterly' and the replacement of Irish Gaelic by English was the most obvious illustration of such change.

But we are running ahead of ourselves. Let us wind the clock back to the early seventeenth century and consider the language situation in Ireland. There were now two mother tongues on the island, Irish and English, and there were four main dialects of English:

- there were speakers of Yola, the old form of English that survived in pockets, especially in Wexford, until the nineteenth century

- there were speakers of Elizabethan and Jacobean English

- there were speakers of Scots, mainly in Ulster

- and there were speakers of Irish, who seem to have grafted English words and structures on to the stem of their Celtic language. In this way, they produced Hiberno-English, a form of English that reflects Irish influence at every linguistic level from the sound patterns and the rhythms, to the vocabulary, the idioms, and the sentence structure.

Elizabethan influences

The second wave of settlers spoke forms of English that had not been standardised. These were richly creative varieties, similar to Shakespeare's, and many people have commented on Ireland's 'good fortune' in receiving the language when its speakers were in one of their most creative and uninhibited periods. John Braidwood, a Scot, makes this point overtly in his analysis of Ulster speech:

> ... *the Irish were fortunate to acquire their English during the uninhibited Elizabethan period, when Irish linguistic taste found a stimulating collaborator in the Elizabethan English* ...

> (J. Braidwood, 'Ulster and Elizabethan English', 1964: 81)

Braidwood's claim encapsulates a truth, but not the whole truth. The Irish had already been exposed to varieties of English long before the Elizabethans arrived. And the loss of a mother tongue, even if it is replaced by the most useful language on the planet, is not a fate to be unequivocally welcomed.

So the second phase of English influence began in the middle of the sixteenth century and was augmented by other waves of settlement. Throughout the reigns of Mary and Elizabeth, English farmers were encouraged to settle, especially in Leix and Offaly. Many of these settlers were Protestants from Devon and Cornwall, and Sir Walter Raleigh, also a west countryman, spent eighteen months in Ireland in 1580–81. During this period, Raleigh developed ideas on colonisation that he put into effect in Virginia and in South America in the late sixteenth and early seventeenth centuries. He practised the art of fortress building in Ireland before setting sail for the Americas. He also introduced a plant into Ireland that had been cultivated in the Andes for at least 3000 years before the birth of Christ. The plant was the potato. It flourished in the Irish climate and became the staple food of the poor, thus indirectly contributing to the dependence on one crop that resulted in a catastrophic famine of 1846–49. (The famine was even harder to bear because, although the potato failed, other crops such as corn were plentiful. Indeed, because of the Corn Laws, passed in Westminster in 1804 to protect English farmers against foreign competition, Irish corn was exported to England in large quantities.)

When James I came to the throne in 1603, the Irish expected much from the son of the executed Catholic, Mary Queen of Scots. James, however, continued the Tudor tradition of planting in Ireland people who were loyal to the Crown. The one major difference is that he rewarded many of his Scottish followers with tracts of land, especially in Ulster.

An extension of the settlement of English speakers in Ireland came in the 1640s. The Irish had remained loyal to Charles I in his struggle with Parliament. (The struggle was also with inflation, a fact that is rarely mentioned. Many prices rose 300% during 1625–49, the reign of Charles I!) In 1649, Charles was executed and troops were sent by Cromwell to subdue the Irish. On 12 September, Drogheda was stormed by General Ireton, and the inhabitants treated with a harshness that was commemorated by Irish people in hundreds of chants, the kindest of which is:

The Pope's in heaven
And Cromwell's in hell
Helping the devil
To ring his big bell.

According to folk tradition, the blood bath in Drogheda was so terrible that even hardened English soldiers asked if the children were also to be put to the sword. The answer was 'yes, because nits grow into lice'. It was not only Drogheda, of course, that suffered. Irish farmers were driven off almost eleven million acres of Ireland's best land, which were then distributed to Protestants who were loyal to England. As far north as Tyrone and Fermanagh:

Every surviving Catholic landowner of Catholic stock lost his property...
(W.R. Hutchinson, *Tyrone Precinct*, 1951: 63)

The living conditions of the Irish were reduced to below subsistence level. Many died of famine or by the sword and the population of under 500,000 that survived probably felt that the dead were the lucky ones.

Many historical figures have been demythologised. Some modern writers suggest that Cromwell was undeserving of the criticisms heaped on him by supporters of the executed Charles I (1649) and of his son, Charles II, who was restored to the throne in 1660. Microsoft's CD-ROM *Encarta 98*, for example, describes Cromwell's exploits in Ireland as follows:

> *In 1649 the English soldier and statesman Oliver Cromwell landed at Dublin, which the Roman Catholic lords had been unable to take. With his well-disciplined forces, 10,000 men of the New Model army, he stormed Drogheda and put its garrison of 2000 men to the sword. A similar Cromwell victory occurred at Wexford. Cromwell's successors, the English soldiers and regicides Henry Ireton and Edmund Ludlow, successfully concluded the war, and a great part of the best land of Munster, Leinster and Ulster was confiscated and divided among the soldiers of the parliamentary army. The Roman Catholics and Royalist landowners were banished to Connaught.*

Interestingly, beside this passage, there is an on-screen passage which reads:

> *English writers have estimated that at least 30,000 were put to death by the Irish, but ...*

The fact that the claim ends with ... suggests that the *Encarta* compilers may have had reservations about the figure.

One is reminded of the astute remark made by Samuel Butler in *Erewhon* in 1872:

> *It has been said that although God cannot alter the past, historians can.*

Remembering 1690

The third and last major Protestant plantation occurred after the Battle of the Boyne in 1690. However, smaller groups of immigrants, mainly from Scotland, continued to take up residence, especially in

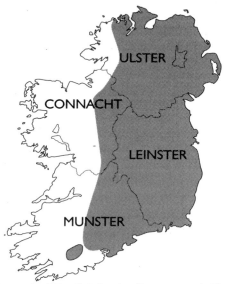

The Spread of English in the Seventeenth Century

Ulster, throughout the eighteenth century. The reason for stressing the religious factor is because this was the first time in history that settlers in Ireland deliberately adopted a policy of segregation along national and religious lines – a policy that was referred to many times in such comments as:

> *Though, in practice, people classify themselves, it was not thought desirable to separate the English and the Scotch; but the Britons generally were kept distinct from the Irish as well for their greater security as to preserve the purity of the English language.*
>
> (A. Hume, *Essays on Down and Antrim*, 1864: 26)

The records of contacts between Ireland and England are littered with details of famine, poverty, massacres, persecution and eviction. The history books offer evidence of treachery from Smerwick in Kerry, through Drogheda and Limerick and Kinsale. They do not offer many comments on language use. The few comments we have, even from English people born in Ireland, are often prejudiced and imprecise, like the following from Jonathan Swift:

> *How is it possible that a gentleman who lives in those parts where the* townlands *(as they call them) of his estate produce such odious sounds from the mouth, the throat, and the nose, can be able to repeat the words without dislocating every muscle that is used in speaking, and without applying the same tone to all other words, in every language he under-stands; as it is plainly to be observed not only in those people of the better sort who live in Galway and the Western parts, but in most counties of Ire-land?... What we call the Irish* brogue *is no sooner discovered, than it makes the deliverer, in the last degree, ridiculous and despised; and from such a mouth, an Englishman expects nothing but bulls, blunders and follies.*

If English with an Irish accent could be so severely stigmatised, we can imagine the contumely that was reserved for speakers of Gaelic.

The term 'Irish Bull' refers to a statement that seems to contain a contradiction. No-one knows where this 'bull' comes from although it may be a form of French *boule*, 'deceit'. Irish bulls are statements like 'You'd be mad to want to live in a lunatic asylum' or 'Childlessness runs in their breed.' A little thought allows one to see that the claims are often true. It was Maria Edgeworth's *Essay on Irish Bulls* (1802) that most clearly associated such statements with the Irish.

The Rose and the Thistle

Because of the specific policies of colonisation adopted towards Ire-land, the Irish from the seventeenth century onward were presented with two main models of English: the English of England and Wales, especially in the southern part of the country, and the English of Scotland, mainly in the north. These varieties have, rather romanti-cally, been referred to as the rose and the thistle, although there was nothing romantic about the spread of either variety.

The linguistic divisions between north and south, which were an accident of history, in that Scotland was closer to Ulster, were reinforced when, in 1921, Ireland was divided into the twenty-six counties of the Irish Free State (*Saorstát Éireann*) (later to become *Poblacht na hÉireann*, the Republic of Ireland) and the six counties of Northern Ireland (which remained British). However, the dialect boundaries are not a perfect match for the political ones. Today, most of the descendants of the Planters in the six counties regard themselves as British and see their future within the United Kingdom. Many in the Catholic community think of themselves as Irish and aspire to some sort of union with the Republic of Ireland. The Republic traditionally maintained the ideal of a united Ireland, an ideal that was enshrined in Articles 2 and 3 of its constitution:

> *The national territory consists of the whole island of Ireland, its islands and territorial seas.*
>
> *Pending the reintegration of the national territory, and without prejudice to the right of the Parliament and Government established by this Constitution to exercise jurisdiction over the whole of that territory, the laws enacted by that Parliament shall have the like area and extent of application as the laws of Saorstát Éireann (i.e. the twenty-six counties of the Republic) and the like extra-territorial effect.*

As a result of the Referendum of 22 May 1998, however, 95 percent of the people who voted in the Republic of Ireland made it clear that they were willing to give up their territorial claims on the six counties of Antrim, Armagh, Derry, Down, Fermanagh and Tyrone unless and until the majority of voters in the six counties wish to rejoin the twenty-six counties of the Republic. The electorate in the six counties was voting on a related issue: whether or not to accept the 'Good Friday Agreement' that would create a power-sharing Assemby in Stormont and a voice in government for both England and the Republic of Ireland. According to the *Sunday Times* (25 May), the Northern Ireland electorate voted as follows:

It is not possible to be totally certain about how the above pattern breaks down but the paper's best estimates were:

Voting by Gender	YES	NO
Women	75%	25%
Men	68%	32%

Voting by Age	YES	NO
18-34	70%	30%
35-44	71%	29%
45-59	76%	24%

The above table was not broken down according to religious preferences although some evidence suggests that Protestant women were more likely to vote 'yes' than were their menfolk.

The Six Counties

The Sounds of Planter English

All speakers of English in Ireland, whether of Irish, English or Scottish ancestry, are currently influenced by education, media norms and the growing prestige of Americanisms. Nevertheless, it is possible to distinguish two main traditions of English on the island: Planter English and Hiberno-English. Planter English is represented by two varieties, namely Anglo-Irish and Ulster Scots. This latter variety is strictly limited to Northern Ireland (including parts of Donegal) and it is often confused with Scots. The reasons for this are immediately apparent in Ulster Scots writings, such as this poem written in Northern Ireland in 1901:

> *The auld gaberlunzie* [beggar] *sae reggit an' spare*
> *That used tae gang leppin alang*
> *Wi' a skep, an a twerl, an' a boon* [bound] *in the air*
> *An' a 'whoop', an' a bedlamite sang. –*
> *'Holy Bridget' they ca'd him, acause as he went,*
> *'Holy Bridget!' a' day wuz his cry,*
> *As he shuck hissel' oot wi' a shiver, an' bent*
> *Tae beg o' the stranger near-by.*

Anglo-Irish

Anglo-Irish is a variety of English spoken over most of Ireland. It is descended from the English brought to Ireland by planters from England, modified by contacts with Irish, Ulster Scots and Hiberno-English.

Like Ulster Scots, Anglo-Irish is really a spectrum of Englishes, influenced by the education, the regional origin of its speakers and the area of settlement. The Anglo-Irish of Kerry, for example, is markedly different from the Anglo-Irish of Fermanagh, partly because the northern variety has been influenced by a different dialect of Irish and by Ulster Scots. Like all varieties of Irish English, it is **rhotic**, that is, the 'r' is pronounced in words like *far* and *farm*. The pronunciation of the 'r' is less rolled than in Ulster Scots. There is also a diminishing tendency, possibly due to influence from Irish, to introduce a short vowel between the 'r' and the following consonant so that *arm* may sound like *aram*.

The majority of Anglo-Irish speakers approximate to network norms although some older, rural and uneducated speakers have retained features of the educated speech of Elizabethan and Jacobean England. Many of the sounds, therefore, that socially-mobile mothers may correct are actually conservative retentions, the pronunciation 'relics of oul' dacency'. We find the almost invariable use of '-in' for '-ing' in 'walking' and other retentions occur in the rhyming of such pairs as:

Perfect		Rhymes
beard	with	heard
cold	with	cowl
fur	with	four
hold	with	howl
meat	with	state
old	with	owl
pea(cock)	with	pay(cock)
tea	with	ray

For many of the same speakers, there is a set of commonly-occurring words that are pronounced with the same vowel sound as *hut*. The most frequently heard of these are:

bull, bullet, bush, butcher
could, cushion
foot, full
look
pull, pullet, push, put
shook
took
wood, wool, would

Some southern speakers have, in the past, tended to pronounce 's' as 'sh', especially in word-final position, so that *dense* occurred as *densh*, and in consonant clusters involving 's', so that 'story' was occasionally pronounced *shtory* and 'small' *shmall*. Similarly, 'z' was sometimes replaced by the initial sound of French *je*, especially when it is followed by 'd' or 'l' or 'n', as in *buzzed* and *drizzle*. It is not certain whether such tendencies were the result of influence from Irish or whether some Elizabethan and Jacobean speakers used such pronunciations. In favour of the second hypothesis is the fact that some varieties of West African English pronounced 's' as 'sh', so that 'small' was realised as *shmall*, 'stick' as *shtick* and 'story' as *shtory*. Of course, even if some English speakers did occasionally pronounce 's' as 'sh', the fact that Irish speakers pronounced *sean*, 'old' as *shan* would have reinforced this tendency.

A short intrusive vowel still sometimes separates a syllable-ending cluster so that *faram* is heard for 'farm' and *filim* for 'film' and, especially in the south-west, the vowel sound in words like 'pen' is often replaced by the vowel in 'pin', thus causing 'pen' and 'pin' to become homophones.

One of the clearest differences between Northern and Southern English is the pronunciation of 'th' as in 'thin' and 'then'. In the south these are often replaced by 't' and 'd' so that 'tin' and 'thin' are near homophones, as are 'den' and 'then'. In educated speech, the sound used, especially at the end of words, is not quite 't' and not quite 'th'. Rather, it is a blend of both so that 'faith' sounds like 'fate + th'.

Ulster Scots

Ulster Scots is a variety of Scottish English spoken mainly in parts of Antrim, Donegal and Down, although its influence can be found as far south as south Tyrone, Armagh and Fermanagh. Like the Lowland Scots from which it came, it is rhotic, and the 'r' is occasionally rolled in words such as 'car' and 'card'. Like most varieties of English, it occurs in a spectrum of forms largely related to a person's education and social position. The lower down the social ladder, the more likely is the speaker to rhyme:

Ulster Scots Perfect Rhymes			Standard English Perfect Rhymes		
blood	with	good	blood	with	mud
cow	with	do	cow	with	bough
die	with	see	die	with	high
ground	with	soon	ground	with	sound
home	with	game	home	with	roam
hot	with	caught	hot	with	cot
so	with	say	so	with	know

Many Ulster Scots speakers also tend to drop the 'l' sound in words such as *call* and *full*; to use a glottal stop instead of 't' in words such as *water* and *got*; to roll the 'r' slightly, especially when it is the first sound in a word, as in *red* and *round*; and to use the guttural sound that linguists call a velar fricative in the pronunciation of words such as *Augher*, *lough* and (horse) *trough*.

A distinction between many Ulster Scots speakers and others in Ireland is that they tend to use the same vowel sound in the words *bull*, *cook*, *foot*, *loose* and *lose*, whereas many speakers of Hiberno-English follow the Anglo-Irish pattern of rhyming *bull* with *gull*, *foot* with *gut*, and *lose* with *toss*.

In *North*, Seamus Heaney draws attention to this pronunciation when he tells us:
I tried to write about the sycamores
And innovated a South Derry rhyme
With hushed *and* lulled *full chimes for* pushed *and* pulled.

Education and media influences are eradicating many of the most markedly regional features from the speech of the young, but it is still true to claim that speakers of Ulster Scots have fewer vowel and more consonant contrasts than speakers of BBC English and, like Irish people generally, use a pronunciation system that is in many ways similar to General American English.

The Words of Planter English

The vocabulary of Irish English has, like its sound patterns, three main sources: English, Scots and Irish Gaelic. Speakers of Anglo-Irish use essentially the same vocabulary as English speakers world-wide, but there are certain features that distinguish their vocabulary from that of the English or the Scots, for example.

In the first place, it has traditionally included items that are either no longer current in the standard language, or have markedly different meanings. It is not that the Anglo-Irish speakers of English got them wrong. Rather, they preserved forms from an earlier period. Shakespeare and his contemporaries knew and used many of the words still found in parts of Ireland. As recently as 1990, I recorded examples of:

Atomy	(small, insignificant person)
crawthumper	(person who is overly religious)
mitch	(play truant)

in Donegal. These were used in contexts that may be compared with citations from earlier periods of English in England:

Irish English	Earlier English
Such an atomy and he had that much to say for himself!	You starved blood-hound! Thou atomy, thou! (2 Henry IV, V.iv.33, 1597)
We were called crawthumpers.	*Craw thumper*, a Roman Catholic (*Slang Dictionary*, 1873)
The boys mitch more than the girls. Girls seem to like school better.	What made the Gods so often to trewant from Heaven, and mych heere on earth... (John Lyly, *Euphues*, 1580)

Others occur with meanings which are different from those in the standard language:

Backward	(shy)
doubt	(suspect, believe: *I doubt it will rain.* = I strongly believe that it will rain.)
thick-witted	(stubborn)

but many of these words are dying out. One of the consequences of a formal education is a standardised vocabulary.

> **There is much excellent writing in Ulster Scots, including W.G. Lyttle's novel *Betsy Gray; or Hearts of Down: A Tale of Ninety-Eight:***
>
> *As Mat finished his song he swung the ponderous hammer around his head with a flourish, and flung it in a corner. Then turning to Gray he said –*
>
> *"What's the matter, Geordie? Why there's no word oot o' yer heid the nicht ava."*
>
> *George smiled sadly as he answered, "I do feel a bit dull, Mat, but I'll be all right in the morning."*
>
> *"Keep up your heart, my boy," said Mat cheerily, as he slapped George on the back with his grimy hand, "the darkest hooer's aye afore daybrek…"*
>
> *Mat held up his finger and shook it reprovingly.*
>
> *"Dinnae be throwin' a wat blanket on me, Geordie, because if a didnae believe that iverything wad gang richt, deil tak the pike a wad mak mair."*
>
> *"Well, you have made a good mank, Mat," remarked George.*
>
> *"Ay, ye may weel say that; if a man that a cud name seen what's hid in "The Moat" he wad tell a gie story in a certain place."*
>
> *"Who do you mean, Mat?"*
>
> *"Wha dae a mean? I'll tell ye that…"*

The similarities between the pronunciation of Ulster Scots and Lowland Scots are reinforced by vocabulary. Although many dialect words are recessive in Ireland, items such as the following can be heard in the natural speech of Ulster Scots speakers, especially those from rural areas.

babby	(baby, child)
bairn	(baby, child)
bogle	(spirit, poltergeist)
blurt	(tell, let out information)
burn	(stream)
fankle	(become tangled)
fash	(anger, worry: *Dinna fash.* = Don't worry, be upset.)

Planter English

fernenst	(in front of)
flit	(move house)
girn	(complain)
greet	(cry: *Dinna greet, hen.* = Don't cry, love.)
jeg	(prick)
jook	(avoid)
lassie	(young girl)
peelywally	(unwell)

Moreover, with Scots now recognised as a minority language by Europe, Scots words are experiencing something of a renaissance in both Scotland and Northern Ireland. This fact should remind us that words can be called back from the dead and given a new lease of life if social conditions warrant it. How many of us realised in the 1980s that *punk* was not a new creation or that in 1603, Shakespeare had written:

She may be a Puncke (Measure for Measure, V.1. 179)

Many claims and counter claims have been made about the vocabulary of Irish English but few of them can readily be put to the test. There are three, however, that are worth emphasising:

1. Although regionalisms are frequently criticised, many non-standard forms are often more 'correct' than those that now occur in the standard language. A few rural examples of dialect forms from Tyrone illustrate their link with the past.

Irish English	Middle English	Standard English
acquent	aqueynt	acquainted
apricock	abricock	apricot
axe	acsian	ask
bagle	bé-gueule	beagle (open throat)
bairn	barn	child
baste	beste	beast, animal
dreep	drepe	drip
elbuck	elbog(a)	elbow

63

Irish English	Middle English	Standard English
entermeddle	entremedle	interfere, meddle
fenster	fen(e)ster	window
kist	kist	chest

2. A number of dialect words in Irish English are of French origin. Most of these probably came in via Scotland, where there is also a considerable French element in the dialect. The tradition of borrowing from French into Scots goes back at least as far as the sixteenth century, when Mary Stuart was Queen of both Scotland and France, and Scottish people had the right to claim French citizenship.

Irish English	French	Standard English
ashet	assiette	large plate
beautique	boutique	up-market shop
bonnet	bonet	cap
brave	brave = fine	fine
dishabels	deshabiller = to undress	night attire
flinch	flenchir = turn aside	be startled
grossarts	groseilles	gooseberries
gutt(h)ery	gotière = muddy	muddy
hogo	haut goût = strong flavour	bad smell
musheroon	mousseron	mushroom
poofee	pouffe	soft footstool

3. Many words that are classified as 'etymology unknown' in the *Oxford English Dictionary* may well come from Irish Gaelic. This phenomenon will be explored further in the following chapter, but a brief table may help to illustrate the point:

Dialect	Meaning	Gaelic	OED etymology	First recorded
boke, puke	retch	piochán	unknown	1600
cadge	get for nothing	goid	unknown	1812
cant	insincere talk	cainnt	unknown	1532
cog	cheat	caog	unknown	1532
crack	joke	cra(i)c	imitative	1450
gammy	lame	cam	unknown	1839
grouse	grumble	gramhas	unknown	1892
puss	face	pus	unknown	1890

Dialect	Meaning	Gaelic	OED etymology	First recorded
spree	romp	spréidh	unknown	1804
twig	understand	tuig	unknown	1815

There are, of course, many scholars, including Irish ones, who will deny that such words are Irish in origin. More than one has argued, passionately, that Irish took 'crack' from English. And they may be right. However, it is interesting to look at some of the earliest uses of these words. *The Oxford English Dictionary* acknowledges that Old English had no noun 'crack' and cites a Scottish quotation as its first example. One of the earliest English examples comes from Edmund Spenser's *Faerie Queene* (1590):

> *Leasinges, backbytinges and vain-glorious crakes.*

but Spenser spent much of his adult life in Ireland.

The Grammar of Planter English

The grammatical structure of all varieties of English in Ireland is influenced by education and the media. Nevertheless, clear differences may be noted that reflect, to some extent, the historical and linguistic backgrounds of the people on the island.

The grammar of uneducated speakers of Anglo-Irish includes many features which are found in other non-standard varieties throughout the world, including the United States, and of course in Hiberno-English. Many people use *done* and *seen* in affirmative, past tense structures:

> *They done their best, so they did.*
> *I never seen it myself now but I know others that seen it.*

Many also favour alternative past tense and past participles, such as *clum*, *took* and *wrought* rather than 'climbed', 'taken' and 'worked' as in:

> *We've clum the hill together.*

65

> *The chile has his exams all took now.*
> *You couldn't fault that man. He wrought hard every day of his life.*

Some continue the Shakespearean tradition of using the same form as both the past tense and the past participle:

> *I have took note of it (Hamlet, V.i.).*

The woman who reported that:

> *I've forgot all the poetry I ever learnt.*

was using the same form that Shakespeare did in his sonnet 'No longer mourn for me when I am dead':

> *... for I love you so,*
> *That I in your sweet thoughts would be forgot,*
> *If thinking on me then would make you woe.*

The same speakers, in casual conversation, often employ *a* + past tense where *have* + past participle would be required in the standard language:

> *She would a went now if you had a asked her.*
> *I might a knew* (known). *He was always cowl* (unadventurous).

Like dialect speakers world-wide, they often use *them* as a demonstrative plural adjective and pronoun:

> *Where did you put them pears?.*
> *Them's mine.* (They are mine.)

They frequently indulge in what linguists call 'negative concord'. What this means is that whereas 'two negatives make an affirmative' in Standard English, two, three or even four negatives are used for emphasis as in:

> *No, he never gave nothin' to nobody.*
> *Well, you'll never see nothin' like them again. Them'ns wouldn't a done nobody no harm.*

The use of negative concord was common in the standard language of the sixteenth and seventeenth centuries and many Irish speakers could echo both the sentiments and the grammar of Shakespeare's conclusion to his sonnet 'Let me not to the marriage of true minds admit impediments':

> *If this be error and upon me proved,*
> *I never writ, nor no man ever loved.*

Most speakers in Ireland use a plural form of *you* to address more than one person. The form used tends to be either *ye*, *yiz* or *youse*:

> *Ye'll be the death of me yet.*
> *Yiz is all on the pig's back.*
> *Youse don't know the half of it!*

It is likely that Irish Gaelic speakers influenced the use of a plural pronoun because Gaelic invariably uses *tú* for 'you singular' and *sibh* for 'you plural'. It is also likely that Irish speakers may have been instrumental in the spread of such a plural as 'youse' in the United States and Australia.

Irish is one of the few remaining languages in Europe to have a singular pronoun *tú* that is always singular and a plural pronoun *sibh* that is always plural. Other languages use the plural pronoun as a form of respect to an individual who is not well known, as in:

> *Bonjour Madame, comment allez-vous?*

rather than the more logical, but less polite:

> *Bonjour Madame, comment vas-tu?*

In English, *thou* used to be the singular pronoun and *you* the plural pronoun that was used as a singular of respect. In *Twelfth Night*, for example, Duke Orsino is addressed as 'you':

> *Will you go hunt, my lord?*

while he addresses his attendant as 'thou':

> *Thou know'st no less but all.*

Gradually, 'you', the pronoun that once implied plurality, was generalised as the only second-person pronoun in English.

Perhaps the way in which rural, uneducated Anglo-Irish speakers use the verb 'to be' is one of their most marked characteristics. They tend to use 'is' and 'was' with plural subjects and with *yiz*, *youse*, *yous'ns* and *them'ns*, but not with *they*, *we* or *you*:

> *John and the childer's in bed.*
> *Me and Peter's of an age.*
> *Yiz is drowned.* (very wet)
> *Them'ns wasn't asked.*

and it is probably true to say that, in informal contexts, non-standard features occur higher up the social ladder in Ireland than in many parts of Britain. I have, for example, recorded teachers in relaxed circumstances saying:

> *Thon eejit would a said anything.*
> *She seen you comin'.* (You were cheated.)
> *Them youngsters has no manners.*

Language performance is strictly monitored, however, on formal occasions, often resulting in what linguists call 'hypercorrections'. These are words and phrases that have been 'corrected'. The vowel sound that occurs in 'mud' and 'shut' has also been used so often in words such as 'foot' that many speakers avoid it, even when it would be correct. Thus, they may substitute 'poodle' for 'puddle' and 'daws' for 'does'. Similarly, '-ing' is so often reduced to '-in' that, occasionally, words like 'garden' and 'warden' are 'corrected' to 'garding' and 'warding'. At the level of grammar, children have so often been taught that 'I done it' is wrong, that they use 'have did' and 'have saw' when they are trying to be on their best linguistic behaviour.

Rhymes and tongue twisters often highlight local pronunciations. Children in parts of Ireland still encourage younger – and more innocent – members of the community to say *I put my foot in a bucket and I footed the bucket about* quickly. Since the children rhyme 'put' and 'foot' with 'shut', they often produce the omnipurpose word, most frequently written *f****.

The grammar of Ulster Scots speakers overlaps Anglo-Irish usage, but many speakers in Northern Ireland also employ constructions that are found only in Scotland and in Scottish communities overseas. These include the use of such Scottish idioms such as:

come speed	(succeed)
stand good for Jack	(act as guarantor for Jack)
trail the wing	(look for sympathy)

and the attachment of *nae/no/ny* as negative markers, especially after *can*, *do* and *will*:

A cannae hear his name an' hide
My thought wi' ony art.
She didny ken what's wrang wi' me.
I'll no be able to do it.

Whereas most dialect speakers in Ireland use 'them' for 'those', Ulster Scots speakers tend to use *they* where 'those' is the accepted standard form:

Where did you put they pears?
They books is me da's.

The Anglo-Irish and Ulster Scots varieties of Planter English have their origins outside the island of Ireland but the hundreds of thousands of English and Scottish immigrants, who settled in Ireland during the sixteenth and seventeenth centuries, began the thrust that resulted in the anglicisation of the country. Their English provided the models for the native Irish population and contributed in no small measure to the entity that we now know as Irish, or Green, English.

CHAPTER FOUR

Hiberno-English

(Dumb,
bloodied, the severed
head now chokes to
speak another tongue –

As in
a long suppressed dream,
some stuttering garb-
led ordeal of my own)

An Irish
child weeps at school
repeating its English.
After each mistake

The master
gouges another mark
on the tally stick
hung about its neck

Like a bell
on a cow, a hobble
on a straying goat.
To slur and stumble

In shame
the altered syllables
of your own name
to stray sadly home

And find
the turf-cured width
of your parents' hearth
growing slowly alien:

In cabin
and field, they still
speak the old tongue.
You may greet no one.

To grow
a second tongue, as
harsh a humiliation
as twice to be born.

Decades later
that child's grandchild's
speech stumbles over lost
syllables of an old order.

(John Montague, 'A Grafted Tongue')

As well as the two varieties of Planter English described in Chapter 3, we find forms of English that are regularly referred to as 'HibernoEnglish'. This is a range of English spoken by people whose ancestral mother tongue was Irish. It is strongest in the vicinity of the Gaeltachts, in rural areas and in parts of the country such as the Sperrin

Mountains in Tyrone, where pockets of Gaelic speakers survived until the 1960s. This is a 'grafted English', at one and the same time comprehensible to other speakers of English and yet still in communion with the Gaelic language that was the mother tongue of its speakers' ancestors. It seems likely that it was more widely spoken in the past, but education and the media are eroding this variety too.

When we stop to think about the phenomenon of language loss, it is often hard to explain why a language ceases to be passed on from one generation to the next. Why did Irish grandmothers or great-grandmothers stop speaking Irish Gaelic to their children as their mothers had done to them for countless generations back? It is a little easier to understand why African-American women passed on a form of English to their children. They were seized from their homes, packed into slave ships and transported to new lands with people who may have shared their condition but not their language. But Irish women stayed at home. They lived with Irish men. They met other Irish people every day and they all spoke the same language. Perhaps a partial answer lies in social conditions. Living conditions for most Irish people, especially in the eighteenth and nineteenth centuries, were appalling. Lady Nugent, the wife of the governor of Jamaica from 1801 to 1805, wrote in her journal for 23 January 1802:

> *Treated them* [i.e. the Jamaican Slaves] *with beef and punch, and never was there a happier set of people than they appear to be. All day they have been singing odd songs, only interrupted by peals of laughter; and indeed I must say, they have reason to be content, for they have many comforts and enjoyments. I only wish the poor Irish were half as well off.*
>
> (ed. Philip Wright, *Lady Nugent's Journal of her Residence in Jamaica from 1801–1805*, 1966: 53)

The potato became the main source of food for Irish people and their interest in the potato is reflected in the many terms applied to it. It is said that the Inuit, often incorrectly referred to as 'Eskimos', have over a hundred words for 'snow' and that Arabs have a similar number for 'sand'.

> The Inuit or Innuit people live in North America and Greenland and are closely related to the Aleut of Asia. The term 'Eskimo' comes from an Inuktitut word meaning 'eater of raw meat' and was applied to the Inuit by outsiders.

The Irish do not have a hundred synonyms for *Solanum tuberosum*, but researchers have recorded such variants as the following and the list is by no means exhaustive.

Graded by size	For planting	Uncooked	Cooked
marley	cutling	potato	boxty
taw	poureen	pritty	brudgy
chat	shaleen	spud	champ
crachan	spachan	taty	prockus

And, in many parts of the world, including West Africa, this root vegetable is known as the 'Irish potato', just as siblings that are very close in age are known as 'Irish twins'.

Separation and power

With the advantage of hindsight, we can say that there were five main reasons why the natural transmission of a language from one generation to the next was disrupted in Ireland:

1. The first may be laid at the door of the second wave of planters. Throughout the sixteenth and seventeenth centuries, hundreds of thousands of settlers from England and Scotland moved to Ireland, and for the first time in the recorded history of sustained contacts we find segregation, not integration. In 1646, with the failure of the Irish rebellion, Sir John Temple, writing in support of King Charles I, advised that the British should take precautions against the Irish and that:

> *... there may be ... such a wall of separation set up betwixt the Irish and the British, as it shall not be in their power to rise up (as now and in all former ages they have done).*

Two hundred years later, in 1864, A. Hume noticed that the separation continued. As recently as 1974, a doctor in Belfast, dealing with traumatised children was so forcibly struck by the differences between Catholics and Protestants in Northern Ireland, that he concluded that the conflict in Northern Ireland was a racial one.

> *Ulster's problem is a racial one, a conflict of cultures and ideals between two ethnic groups as distinct as are Blacks and Whites in the United States or Southern Africa. In at least one respect the two groups are, in fact, even more distinct, since mixed marriage, always the exception in Ulster, is now so uncommon as to rate Romeo and Juliet treatment in local news media.*
>
> *Community inbreeding, jut like inbreeding in a family, emphasizes and exaggerates unique characteristics. The end result in Ireland, after three centuries, is two races that contrast physically, emotionally and ideologically. At extremes the Celtic group have darker hair and eyes, more swarthy complexions and more angular features than their Anglo-Saxon counterparts, as well as an accent with longer vowel sounds and softer consonants. The accent difference, as well as being an expression of varying geographical roots, may also reflect something of the importance laid on the Irish language in Catholic Schools.*
>
> *These physical and accent differences, although by no means universal, are still sufficient to enable most Ulster Catholics or Protestants to identify one another on sight.*
>
> (Morris Fraser, *Children in Conflict*, 1974: 115–6)

2. Secondly, although closely linked with the previous point, there were the punitive penal laws of the eighteenth century. These laws were designed to enshrine the powers and privileges of an English elite, and they reduced the native population of Ireland to subsistence level. The Irish language could not be used as a medium for anyone interested in educational, economic or political advancement.

3. A third nail in the coffin of the Irish language was the system of National Schools introduced in 1831. The sole medium of education in these schools was English. Children were punished, like the child in Montague's poem, if they used Irish. These schools promoted a policy of language shift by their 'unrelenting determination to stamp out the Irish language' (Douglas Hyde, *A Literary History of Ireland*, 1967: 632).

This is how the Penal Laws were described in a widely-used history book. The book was used in primary school by my mother, but the phenomenon of a horse for £5 was part of Ireland's mythology even in the 1980s. Eamonn McCann referred to it in *War and an Irish Town*, 1980. Part of the text book reads:

> *After peace was restored to Ireland, a Parliament was called at Dublin. The first business done was the passing of the terms of an oath, which all members were required to take. In this oath it was declared that the Roman Catholic doctrines were false. As no Roman Catholic could take such an oath, those of that religion were thus prevented from sitting in parliament. In that and successive parliaments were passed many harsh laws penalising Roman Catholics ....*

> *By the penal laws ... Roman Catholic schoolmasters were prohibited from teaching, and Roman Catholic parents were forbidden to send their children to a foreign country for education in their own religion.*

> *No Catholic could have a horse of greater value than £5, i.e. £30 of our money.*

> *All parish priests had to be registered, whilst Roman Catholic bishops and religious orders were banished.*

> *Laws were then passed ... which penalised the Irish in their export trade. A heavy duty was put on exported wool ... Other export traffic from Ireland ... was either prohibited or hindered, so that many Irish industries were greatly crippled, and many people were thrown out of employment. The people of Ulster suffered most in the loss of trade, though they were Protestants, and many thousands of the Ulster Scots left Ireland and emigrated to America.*

> (R. McIlroy, *A Concise History of the Stuart Period*, specially written for pupils in National Schools, n.d: 68–9)

4. Fourthly, there was the 'Great Hunger' of 1846–49. No one is certain how many people died in this famine because no one really knows exactly how large the native population in Ireland was in the eighteenth and early nineteenth centuries. It is likely, however, that it was in the region of eight million by 1845. Whatever the precise figure, Cecil Woodham-Smith suggests (*The Great Hunger* 1962: 411) that as many as one third of the population perished. If one in three people died, it is no wonder that the remaining two thirds thought that both their land and their culture were doomed.

5. The fifth reason is the one that is explored in this chapter. It is a partial linguistic reason for the abandonment of a mother tongue by so many. From the beginning of the seventeenth century, many Irish speakers began to communicate with English speakers by grafting English words and structures onto the stem of their Celtic language. This is a technique that linguists call 'relexification'. In relexification, a person learns some words from a target language but slots them in to the grammatical patterns of their mother tongue. Relexification is not an unusual process. We see it in the mistakes children make when they translate English into French, as in the following examples taken from GCSE papers:

English	'Translation'	Target French
I am going home	Je suis allant chez moi	Je vais chez moi
he likes her	il aime la	il l'aime
covered with clouds	couvert avec nuages	couvert de nuages
my brother's car	mon frère's auto	l'auto de mon frère

Relexification is widespread in communities where one group of people tries to learn the language of another under conditions of pressure or segregation. By this process, the Irish produced a form of English that reflected Irish influence at every linguistic level from the sound patterns and the rhythms, to the vocabulary, the idioms, and the sentence structure. This 'grafting' produced what we know today as Hiberno-English.

The Sounds of Hiberno-English

At one and the same time, a person's accent is the easiest linguistic feature to detect and the hardest to describe. If we think about it, we would probably all agree with the New Zealand linguist, G.W. Turner, who claims:

> *The total accent can ... no more be described in words than the taste of a banana...*
>
> (*The English Language in Australia and New Zealand*, 1966: 89)

An accent is also, perhaps, the last remnant of a former mother tongue to be relinquished. If we see, for example, the comments of an Irish politician quoted in the newspaper, they are often indistinguishable in form from the expression of similar sentiments by a Scot or an American. When we hear Irish politicians speak, on the other hand, the accent is an immediate indication of their country of origin.

When, as part of a linguistic experiment, a group of English students were asked to describe an Irish lecturer's accent, they came up with such claims as:

- 'it has more ups and downs than an English accent', that is, the intonation is more varied, more 'sing song' than someone speaking BBC English

- 'words like *day*, *face*, *gain*, *sail* and *take* sound shorter', that is, such words tend to be pronounced with a long /e/ sound

- '*grass* rhymes with *gas*'

- 'the 'r' is pronounced in words like *car*, *cart* and *course*', that is, the accent is 'rhotic'

- 'it is more correct (!) than BBC English because *witch* is not pronounced the same as *which* and the words *paw*, *poor* and *pour* are all pronounced differently, whereas they sound the same in BBC English'

- 'the sound 'l' is lighter in words such as *call* and *full*'

- 'the sound 't' at the end of words like *let* and *light* is not cut off immediately but almost has a short vowel after it'.

> The terms 'BBC English' and 'the Queen's English' are sometimes used to refer to standard British English with an RP accent. RP, or 'Received Pronunciation', is often regarded as a prestige, educated, British accent. Most accents provide insights into the regional origins of a speaker, but RP is not restricted to any one area of Britain. It is the accent used by the BBC for important, national announcements.

The above comments were all made in a spirit of courtesy and many of the features picked out are indeed widespread in Hiberno-English and seem to have a Gaelic ancestry. The comment about the pronunciation of words such as 'day' and 'gain' is specially insightful. This particular vowel sound has always been pronounced differently in Ireland and England. It was no accident that the Irish playwright George Bernard Shaw selected the sentence:

The rain in Spain stays mainly on the plain.

Eliza Doolittle might say:

The rine in Spine sties minely on the pline

while Hiberno-English speakers do indeed tend to use a longer version of the vowel that occurs in the word 'head'.

When we learn a language as adults, we generally carry over the sounds and rhythms of our mother tongue to the new language. If we think of how most of us might pronounce *joie de vivre* or *enfant terrible* or any French phrase, we realise that the tracks laid down for speaking our mother tongue obtrude into our realisation of French. The same thing happened when our Irish forebears learnt English. They used Irish patterns in the realisation of English. Often this worked well. The short Irish vowels could be used in such English words as 'bill', 'get', 'lad', 'not' and 'nut' and the long Gaelic vowels became an approximate fit for the vowel sounds in 'be', 'gain', 'law', 'no' and 'moon'. The initial consonants in Irish *beag*, 'small', *colm*, 'dove', *fear*, 'man' and *mála*, 'bag', could be used in such English words as 'big', 'call', 'fall', 'go' and 'man'. Other Irish consonants were similar but by no means identical to English ones. These were the sounds 't', 'd', 'l', 's', 'z', 'n' and 'r' and they helped to create a recognisably Irish accent.

In RP, these sounds are made by bringing the tip of the tongue into contact with the ridge behind the top teeth. This is called the *alveolar* ridge and the sounds in English are classified as 'alveolar sounds'. In Irish, the sounds are usually 'dental'. That means that the tip of the tongue tends to come into contact with the back of the top teeth. This may seem like a trivial difference – and it is rarely enough to cause misunderstanding – but when we realise that 't', 'd', 'l', 's', 'z' and 'n' are the most frequently used consonants in English, then we begin to understand that hundreds of tiny differences can add up to a major distinction.

... it is clear that this vowel system [i.e. the system for Irish English] corresponds very closely to the range of phonetic qualities associated with the vowel system of Irish – as spoken, for example, in places as far apart as County Cork ... and County Mayo ... Thus the short vowels /ɪ, ɛ, æ, ɒ, ʌ, ʊ/ correspond to those of Irish *min, deich, fear, mar, deoch, muc,* and the long monophthongs /iː, eː, aː, ɔː, oː, uː/ to those of *mín, féin, meán, fáth, bó, rún.* Unstressed /ə/ is heard in the first and last syllables of such words as *galánta* and the /aɪ,aʊ/ in *leigheas* and *leabhar* respectively.

So there is a measure of truth in the view that an Irish accent consists in the sounds of Irish imposed upon English ...

(J.C. Wells, *Accents of English 2: The British Isles*, 1982: 419)

When the sound 'r' followed 't' or 'd' in Irish, the sounds combined into what linguists have called *interdental affricates*. Needless to say, Irish speakers carried such a technique over from words such as *trácht*, 'mention', *tré*, 'through', *dreige*, 'meteor', and *dris*, 'bramble', into 'try' and 'dry' or 'better' and 'thunder'. And the phenomenon has been highlighted as a feature of Irish pronunciation by writers from the seventeenth century to the present day with such spelling as 'dhry', 'thry', 'betther' and 'thundther'.

Mary: *The full details are in it this mornin'; seven wounds he had – one entherin' the neck, with an exit wound beneath the left shoulder-blade; another in the left breast penethratin' the heart, an...*
Johnny: *Oh, quit that readin' for God's sake! Are yous losin' all your feelin's? It'll soon be that none of you'll read anythin' that's not about butcherin'!*

(Seán O'Casey, *Juno and the Paycock*, 1985 Ayling ed.)

Three other sounds often mark out Irish speakers from their English counterparts. These are 'th' as in 'thing', 'th' as in 'that' and 's' as in 'stick'. In fact, many Irish people do substitute their dental 't' and 'd' for the two English dental sounds represented by 'th'. The story of 's' is, however, much more complex. Speakers of Irish used 'sh' as a variant of 's' in certain contexts. For example, in Irish Gaelic, 's' was pronounced 'sh' when followed by an 'e' or an 'i' as in *sean*, 'old', or *sin*, 'that', but pronounced as a dental 's' when followed by 'a', 'o' 'u' as in *sásta*, 'satisfied', *solus*, 'light', and *suas*, 'up'. Of course, as we saw in Chapter 3, 'sh' was also used for 's' in some early forms of West African English and so, unless we hypothesise that many of the early sailors were Irish, we must consider the possibilities that some English speakers of the period used 'sh' for 's' or that the same linguistic phenomenon can occur in two places without the need to assume a link.

North and South

So far, this account has concentrated on the features of Hiberno-English that are found throughout Ireland, but this is only part of the story. Almost any listener would acknowledge that a rural speaker from west Kerry, for example, could not be confused with one from north Derry. The rhythms, especially, are different in that the Kerry speaker often has the singsong patterns found also in parts of Wales and of the Caribbean. Most rural speakers from Kerry are linguistically closer to Gaelic-speaking ancestors than are their counterparts in Derry. In addition, they tend to reflect the melodies of the south-western dialect of Gaelic rather than the tunes of Ulster Gaelic, which have been overlaid with Scots. It is also true, however, that it is less easy to distinguish between a speaker from adjacent areas of Fermanagh and Cavan. As in other parts of the English-speaking world, there is an unbroken continuum of speech patterns from the northernmost point of Donegal to the southernmost tip of Cork, from the furthest point west in Mayo to the shore of Belfast Lough. The extreme points may be markedly different but there are no sharp distinctions or cut-off points between them.

In general terms, Northern Hiberno-English is found north of an imaginary line that links Dundalk with Bundoran. South of this imaginary line we have Southern Hiberno-English. It is worth noting that this imaginary line does not correspond with any institutionalised boundaries and does not match the lines established for the six counties in 1921 or even for the nine counties of the traditional province of Ulster. The influence of Scots is rare south of this line and strongest in the coastal counties of Northern Ireland. However, it has had a degree of influence on all forms of English north of this line.

Linguistic Boundary

The influence of Scots was augmented in the North by the speech of planters from Northern England and by Ulster Gaelic, itself closer in many ways to Scots Gaelic than to the other main Irish dialects, those of Munster and Connaught. The Irish counties to the south of our imaginary line were influenced mainly by the English of southern

England and of Wales. No single sound can illustrate the difference
between North and South but a fairly reliable shibboleth concerns
the realisation of 'r' in combination with 't' and 'd'.

English	North	South
three trees	three threes	tree trees
father	fa'er	fedther
order	ordther	ardther

Many of the other sounds that are thought of as Irish are shared
between North and South and with other accents of English, including
Anglo-Irish. These include the use of /aul/, as in 'owl', for 'old' as in:

boul(d)	bold
coul(d)	cold
houl(d)	hold
toul(d)	told

and the use of the sound in 'say' rather than 'see' in words such as:

bate	beat
chate	cheat
pace	peace
spake	speak

Yet, both these pronunciations were once found in the speech of the
noblest speakers in England. An Irish woman today offering a visitor
'a cup of tay' would be using a pronunciation in no way distinguishable
from that of Queen Anne (1702–14):

> *Here thou, great Anna! whom three realms obey*
> *Dost sometimes counsel take – and sometimes Tea.*

> (Alexander Pope, *The Rape of the Lock*, III, 1712)

And, if we look at the rhymes used by some English poets of the seventeenth
century, we will find 'soul' rhyming with 'owl', 'sea' rhyming
with 'say', and 'reserve' rhyming with 'starve'. What critics often disparage
as 'mispronunciations' are conservative preservations. Irish
speakers imitated the pronunciations they heard, as closely as they
could. The name 'Keats' began to rhyme with 'sheets' in England but,

in Ireland, 'Yeats' continued to be rhymed with 'dates', its seventeenth-century pronunciation.

Hiberno-English speakers often approximate to the Ulster Scots or to the Anglo-Irish norms of an area, but certain features of Gaelic are preserved. These include the tendency to pronounce 'c' and 'g' as if they were followed by a 'y', so that *cat* sounds like 'kyat' and *garden* like 'gyarden'. Often, too, names like *Hugh* are pronounced as if they began with a 'k'. In Irish, names did not begin with the sound 'h' although names such as 'Colm' had an address form that sounded like 'a hollom'. Thus, if someone spoke to Colm and said:

Colm, wait for me.

it would be:

A Choilm, fan liomsa.

and the name would be pronounced 'hollom'. When Irish speakers first encountered 'Hugh', they would probably have assumed that 'Hugh' was the address form of 'Kyugh' in exactly the same way as 'Hollom' was the address form of 'Colm'. This explanation may also account for the 'kyooze' pronunciation of 'Hughes' and for the less frequent use of 'kyuge' for 'huge'.

The Rhythms of Hiberno-English

Another way of illustrating that speakers of Irish carried over their habitual speech patterns into English is to concentrate for a moment on what can be called 'rhythmic retentions'. This phenomenon, which has not been widely studied, is almost certainly found in other communities where a language shift has occurred. It is a feature, for example, of African-American English, in which the African rhythms and speech patterns continue to be found.

Speakers of Irish carried over into Hiberno-English many of the rhythms of their Gaelic mother tongue. Among the most marked of these is the use of an unstressed *an* at the beginning of a question, as in the following recorded examples:

> *An* what do you have to do to get one?
> *An* can the crossing be rough?
> *An* does your feet not be foundhered? [i.e. cold and wet]
> *An* what about food?

This an coincided with English 'and' but it is also a carry-over from Gaelic, where many yes/no questions begin with the unstressed syllable 'an':

An é sin é?	(Is that it?)
An bhfuil tú ag dul?	(Are you going?)
An maith leat í?	(Do you like her?)

Native speakers of Irish Gaelic would naturally have felt the need for an Irish rhythm even when speaking English. To Irish speakers the *an* might have indicated a question, whereas English listeners would have thought of it as an unstressed 'and'. There would have been no confusion because both sets of speakers would have interpreted it according to the patterns of their mother tongue.

Again, it may be worth stressing that such fortuitous resemblances are not uncommon in language contacts. In some forms of West African English, for example, the word for 'woman' is *uman* or *wuman*. Clearly, if we know nothing about the local African languages, this word seems to come straight from English 'woman'. However, an Efik word *uman* means 'woman' and we have a chance resemblance that reinforced the form and meaning of a particular word.

A second marked form of retained rhythm in Hiberno-English is found in the avoidance of 'yes/no' answers. Irish Gaelic is almost unique among Indo-European languages in not having distinct words for 'yes' or 'no'. Of course, speakers of Irish had methods of indicating affirmation and negation:

An maith leat í?	(Do you like her?)
Is maith.	(= yes)
Ní maith.	(= no)

but they varied with the verb of the original question:

An dtuigeann tú?	(Do you understand?)
Tuigim.	(= yes)
Ní thuigim.	(= no)

If you listen carefully, especially to older speakers of Hiberno-English even today, you will notice how rare it is for them to answer a question with a monosyllable. This phenomenon is so widely recognised that it hardly needs to be illustrated. The following samples from live speech, however, show how it works in practice:

Q: *Did you never think of going?*   A: *Houl' yir whisht, I did not.*
Q: *And can the crossing be rough?*   A: *Rough enough, God knows.*
Q: *An does your feet not be foundered?* A: *Foundered and cut to ribbons.*

Younger people often use 'yes' or 'no' but frequently followed by an explanation, as in:

Q: *Did you pass all your exams?*   A: *Yes I did.*
Q: *Can you see what time it is?*   A: *No I can't.*

Interestingly, these speakers also tend to repeat the verb of the question in their answers, just as their ancestors would have done when speaking Gaelic.

Another example of rhythmic retention occurs in the use of tags that echo Gaelic tags. Perhaps the best-known of these are 'at all at all' and 'surely':

I have no sugar at all at all.

A Gaelic equivalent is *ar chor ar bith*, which is rhythmically identical to 'at all at all'.

Níl siucra agam ar chor ar bith.

Irish Gaelic had many words and phrases that acted as emphasisers, words such as *maise* and *cinnte*, which are paralleled by 'indeed' and 'surely' in Hiberno-English:

Q: *Will you help out?*   A: *I will, surely.*
Q: *Would you like a cuppa?*   A: *I would indeed.*

and many of the others are religious in derivation, coming from such expressions as *Dia linn*, 'God [be] with us', or *le cúnamh Dé*, 'with [the] help of God':

Q: *Were they all injured?*   A: *They were, God help us.*
Q: *Will you be going?*   A: *I will, with the help of God.*

Although the 'God-centred' nature of many Hiberno-English expressions can be traced to Irish Gaelic, it also found its way into AngloIrish, at even the highest levels. Lady Maria Nugent's Jamaica Journal (1801–5) is peppered with them:

Sept. 29th, 1801
... he suffers in mind, though, thank God, not yet in body.
June 17th, 1802
God grant it ...
Nov. 17th, 1803
Thank God! our family have been unusually healthy hitherto.
Dec. 13, 1803
... next time, if I live, please God!

The last feature to be highlighted here is the use of a preposition + pronoun at the end of a sentence, as in the following recorded utterances:

The feet was cut off me and I'd a terrible cold on me.
I've a terrible thirst on me. I could drink the Jordan dry.
She ran into me with her shopping trolley and cut the leg o' me.
(= cut my leg)
His head's at him again. (His headache is back.)

The explanation for this usage is both grammatical and rhythmic. The Celtic languages all combine prepositions and pronouns and use them with the BE-verb in order to structure ideas that are expressed differently in English. So, whereas English speakers say:

A number of sociologists have suggested that English people are the least interested in religion in Europe. If such commentators are right, then the lack of interest in religion may be linked to language. And we might wonder whether English is singularly unsuited to religious expression. If we think of almost anything to do with Christianity, we are struck by two facts:

- English borrowed much of its Christian vocabulary, such as 'charity', 'grace' and 'pious'

- the meanings have been weakened. 'Charity' is no longer necessarily something one would like to receive; 'grace' suggests elegant movement rather than an unmerited favour from God; and it is hard to think of an occasion when it would be a compliment to be described as 'pious'. Even when English uses a word like 'silly' from Old English, it has lost its original meaning of 'holy' and taken on overtones of 'lacking in good sense'.

I'm hungry and he's thirsty.

or:

She's got a dog and they've got a cat.

Gaelic speakers say:

Tá ocras orm agus tá tart air. (lit. be hunger on+me and be thirst on+him)

Tá madadh aici agus tá cat aca. (lit. BE dog at+her and BE cat at+them)

These combined prepositions and pronouns are an integral part of all the Celtic languages and their speakers often feel the need to reflect this usage in English.

A Welsh weather presenter for the ITV (Independendent Television) company regularly sums up with *It will be a cold old day of it.* The 'of it' is unnecessary except, perhaps, for the rhythm.

It is, of course, a well-recognised pedagogical principle that speakers of one language carry over their patterns of pronunciation and their rhythms to another language. This is especially true when they learn the second language as adults and retain, at first, their mother tongue for intimate communication. However, such rhythmic patterns continue to distinguish the speech of those whose first language is now a form of English, but whose ancestral mother tongue was Irish Gaelic. It is an interesting comment on speakers' attitudes to Hiberno-English that many of its older speakers say that they 'talk Irish' not 'English'. Indeed, research shows that such speakers tend to use similar rhythms and intonation patterns when speaking both English and Irish. Such rhythmic retentions from Irish are also most apparent in phatic utterances, questions, idioms, exclamations and prayers:

Hiberno-English	Irish Gaelic	Rhythm
How are you doing?	Conas atá tú	|x x|x
Sure the death's on him.	Tá an bás aige	x x | x x
Bad cess to yiz!	Droch-ádh oraibh	| | x x
a 1,2,3	a h-aon, dó, trí...	x | | |

The Words of Hiberno-English

The vocabulary of Irish English has, like its sound patterns, three main sources: English, Scots and Irish Gaelic. As we might expect, the vocabulary of Hiberno-English speakers contains many words that were taken directly from Irish Gaelic and many more where the form may be English but the meaning reflects the semantics of Irish. The commonest Gaelic retentions are found in the areas of culture:

Hiberno-English	Gaelic origin	Meaning
alanna	a leanbh	child, darling
banshee	bean + sí	fairy woman
boron	bodhrán	hand-held drum
brachag	bratóg	rag (to ward off evil)
bummin'	boman	boasting

Hiberno-English	Gaelic origin	Meaning
cairn	carn	sacred stone mound
camogie	camógaí	game like hockey or hurling
clannish	clann	cliquish
(quare) fake	féach	look of cancer

in the domain of farming:

Hiberno-English	Gaelic origin	Meaning
bog	bog = soft	marsh, marshy land
bonnyclobber	bainne clabar	curds
brach	bruch	halo round moon foretelling bad weather
brock	broc	refuse (noun)
brosny	brosnaí	faggots, sticks
clachan	clachán	strip of land
coolygullen	cuileóg an lín	earwig
creel	críol	basket
culchee, culchie	coillteach	someone from the back of beyond

with regard to food:

Hiberno-English	Gaelic origin	Meaning
bannock	bannóg	homemade bread cake
Barmbrack/barn brack	bairghean breac	bread with fruit in it
boxty	bacstaí	reheated leftovers
caulcannon	cál ceann fhionn	cabbage with butter
croobeen	crúibín	pig's foot
dullice	duileasc	edible seaweed
farl	faráil	type of bread
fraughan	fraochán	wild blue berry
meskin	meascan	crock of butter

and, especially with regard to social interaction. The entire English-using world has heard of *ceilidhe* and *craic* but these are the tip of the iceberg. No two speech communities share the same world view. Irish Gaelic speakers did not change their cultural perspective when they switched to English. Rather, they modulated English to suit the rhythms and, where that was not possible, they kept their own words or direct translations:

Hiberno-English	Gaelic origin	Meaning
asthore	a stór	darling
bat	bata	bat, stick, slap
ceili	céilí	evening visit
coracle	curach	boat
flahool	flaithiúil	generous
galore	go leór	plenty
great	go mór	very friendly
keeny	caoineadh	cry for the dead
poteen	poitín	illicitly brewed alcohol
shannach	seanchaidheacht	comfortable gossip

It would be fair to say that some of these words are also found in Scots, but perhaps we should remember the words of James Wilson in *Lowland Scotch* (1915: 11), where he suggests that some so-called Scottish words may, in fact, come from Scots Gaelic:

> *The absorption of Celtic blood is still in progress. The Gaelic surnames which are common in Strathearn show that the ancestors of many of its inhabitants came from across the Highland line; and what happens now has no doubt been going on for centuries. A Highlander, whose native tongue is Gaelic, and therefore quite unintelligible to his Scotch speaking neighbours, comes down from his ancestral home north of the Grampians, and settles down in some Lowland village, perhaps marrying a Lowland wife. He gradually picks up the dialect of the people among whom he lives, but never entirely forgets the Gaelic he spoke when he was a boy, and speaks Scotch with a Gaelic accent and some Gaelic words and idioms.*

The influence of Gaelic on Irish English is not, of course, limited to a set of words for which English had no equivalent. It is much deeper than that. People may give up their ancestral language and yet cling to its patterning for centuries.

The semantic influence of Gaelic can, as we might expect, be seen in the use of:

1. Irish-inspired metaphors:

He'll put it on the long finger (= postpone something).
Cuireann sé é ar an mhéar fhada [puts he it on the finger long]

2. Similes:

as often as fingers and toes (= often, up to twenty times)
comh minic le méaranna coise agus láimhe [as often with fingers of foot and hand]

3. Idioms which use English words to reflect Gaelic ideas. Perhaps the simplest way to illustrate this is by looking at two expressions involving 'eye':

I got a thorn in the eye of me thumb (=central point of the ball of the thumb)
súil na h-ordóige [eye of the thumb]
That one has the heavy eye on her (= has the power to wish bad luck on someone]
súil throm [eye heavy = evil eye)

4. Proverbs, pithy sayings, the use of subjunctives and the frequent references to God and religion:

Them that rared you was fond of childer (= you're very hard to like)
A dacinter man never faced the clay.
That you may never know want. (May you always have everything you need.)
That you may always have full and plenty.
If God spares me, I'll go the morrow.

This does not mean, of course, that the structures illustrated above could not occur in the speech of an Ulster Scots or an Anglo-Irish speaker. The communities have, after all, lived in the same country for four centuries and it would be most unusual if the influence was all one-way traffic. Nor does it mean that such structures do not occur elsewhere in the English-speaking world. It is simply acknowledging that Irish Gaelic has affected the speech of the original natives of Ireland in much the same way that African languages have influenced the English of Creole-speaking West Indians. Another example would be the way that the languages of the Indian subcontinent can be detected in the speech of children born in Bradford or Leeds, whose parents or grandparents spoke Hindi or Gujerati or Urdu.

Above, we referred to the word 'culchee', which is still widely used in Ireland. In Frances Molloy's novel, *No Mate for the Magpie* (1985: 140), for example, we find the word used in her description of getting on the wrong bus in Dublin:

> *While a was gettin' aff at the other en' a asked the conductor could he direct me te me brother's digs an' when a gave him the address he toul me it was fifteen miles away. A toul him that an oul wan had toul me te take a number nineteen bus an' that that was what a had done. He toul me that a had got the right bus, only it was goin' the wrong direction. A asked him what the hell the number nineteen bus was doin', goin' in the wrong direction. He started to roar an' laugh at me an' said te the driver, we've got a right culchie here, Mick.*

Like many words, the etymology of this is not certain. It may come, as suggested, from a word meaning 'wooded area' and so carry overtones of 'backwoods'. It could also, however, have a much more intriguing origin. It may come from 'Culdee' (Cultor Dei), a member of an Irish-Scottish religious group. Alcuin (735–804), who was an English theologian and advisor to Charlemagne, described the Culdee, as *pueri egyptiaci*, 'children of the Egyptians'. It is impossible to be certain whether he meant that the Celtic Church was descended literally or spiritually from the Egyptian Coptic church but, according to William Dalrymple (*From the Holy Mountain*, 1998: 419):

> *The Irish Litany of saints remembers 'the seven monks of Egypt [who lived] in Disert Uilaig on the west coast of Ireland.'*

The Grammar of Hiberno-English

As far as grammar is concerned, David Greene (*The Irish Language*, 1966: 31) aptly called Gaelic 'a noun-centred language' and this predisposition has been carried over into Hiberno-English. Contemporary linguists would say that Gaelic speakers prefer 'nominal' to 'verbal' structures. That often means that Hiberno-English speakers show a preference for:

Hiberno-English	Gaelic	English
Give me the full of it.	Tabhair domh an lán de.	Fill it
I went the length of the gate.	Chuaidh mé fhad le geata.	I went as far as the gate.
Put ears on you.	Cuir cluasa ort.	Listen attentively.
He got his death.	Fuair sé bás.	He died.
I can't hear my ears.	Níl focal i gcluais le cluineadh agam.	I can't hear.
She got a peep at it.	Fuair sí spléachadh air.	She glimpsed it.

Many of the recorded sentences already used show another feature of Hiberno-English, namely an un-English use of prepositions + pronouns, already referred to in the section on rhythmic retention. This type of structure parallels Gaelic patterns, as we can see from the following examples:

Hiberno-English	Gaelic	English
He lost me book on me.	Chaill sé mo leabhar orm.	He lost my book
I've three years on her.	Tá trí bliana agam uirthi.	I'm three years older than she is.
I let a scrake out o' me.	Leig mé scréach asam	I screamed.
My head's always at me.	Bíonn mo cheann i gcónaí ag cur orm.	I always have a headache.
She took the foot off me.	Bhain sí an chos uaim.	She stepped on my foot.

Foregrounding, a technique whereby words and phrases can be highlighted, is widely practised in Hiberno-English, as it is in Gaelic:

It's Irish he uses when he's travelling around scrounging votes.

(Brian Friel, *Translations*, 1980: 25)

Fine girl you are!
It's Mary wants the book.
It wasn't to make trouble we came.
It's badly failed he is now.

Another example would be the use of emphatic pronouns:

And how's the old man himself?

(Brian Friel, *Translations*, 1980: 26)

93

It's meself was the quare runner.
It's themselves they mus' blame.
Was it himself that come?
Well now, me myself I do it this road.

> There is an interesting parallel between the foregrounding in Hiberno-English structures and in some found in the Caribbean, such as: *Iz Mieri waan di buk* = It's Mary wants the book. Of course, English also has the ability to foreground as in 'It's Mary who wants the book' but the Creole structure is closer in form to Hiberno-English.

In contemporary usage, the reflexive pronoun is often replaced by the rhythmically similar 'your man' or 'your one':

I'm lookin' for your man.
Have you seen him?
Who? Oh, your one!

In writing a chapter like this, one is reminded of the concluding verses of St John's Gospel:

And there are also many other things which Jesus did, the which, if they should be written every one, I suppose that even the world itself could not contain the books that should be written. (21: 25)

If we were to describe all the features of Hiberno-English, we could fill several books, and even then, our efforts would be no more than two-dimensional virtual reality when measured against the linguistic patterns that determine what individuals perceive in their language-created worlds.

Only three remaining features, therefore, will be mentioned, each of which has been carried around the world by Irish speakers in life and in literature.

1. 'After + verb + ing' is used to indicate a recently performed action:

I'm after seein him.

means 'I have just seen him'. This parallels Irish Gaelic, where the means of indicating a recently completed action is carried by a construction that is the equivalent of 'after + verbal noun'. We find this structure used to indicate an Irish speaker in the drama of George Farquhar (1678–1707):

> *Do you be after putting the Count in the Closet.*

> (*The Beaux Stratagem*, 1707)

Farquhar does not get the usage quite right in that his Irish character implies the future, not the recent past. It is possible, however, that Farquhar was using a stage Irishism, already well known when he wrote *The Beaux Stratagem*, because he himself was Irish and was reputed to have fought, as a boy, at the Battle of the Boyne in 1690!

2. Writers characterise an Irish speaker by using 'and + pronoun + verb + ing' to indicate that two actions occurred at the same time:

> *He came in and him singin.*
> *She walked out an him talkin.*

These are calques, or direct translations, of Irish Gaelic and the construction is a favourite of J.M. Synge (1871–1909) in his attempt to recreate peasant Gaelic speech:

> *You'll not be getting your death with me, lady of the house, and I knowing all the ways a man can put food in his mouth.*

> (*The Shadow of the Glen*, 1968 ed.)

3. The final feature is the Irish use of forms of the verb 'to be'. If a Standard English speaker says:

> *Mary is going to school.*

it might imply either:

> *At this very moment, Mary is on her way to school.*

or:

> *Mary is five so she started attending school in September.*

If the same speaker said:

Mary goes to school.

it could imply:

Mary regularly goes to school (although she might be at home at the moment).

English:	*Mary goes to school.* *Mary is going to school.*
French:	*Marie va à l'école.* = Mary goes/is going to school.
Irish:	*Téann Máire ar scoil.* *Tá Máire ag dul ar scoil.* *Bíonn Máire ag dul ar scoil.*
Swedish:	*Maria går till skolen.* = Mary goes/is going to school.

Standard English speakers thus have two methods of suggesting current actions and regularity of action, whereas a French speaker could imply all three of the above meanings by the single sentence:

Marie va à l'école.

English is usually described as a Germanic language with a large Romance element. (The previous sentence, for example, has thirteen words, six of which, namely *usually*, *described*, *language*, *large*, *Romance* and *element*, are from Latin via French.) Yet, none of the Germanic languages or French or Latin distinguishes between such sentences as:

Mary is going to school.
Mary goes to school.

The Celtic languages, on the other hand, make a tripartite distinction, one that is not easy to describe in English because the English language does not make it. In Irish Gaelic, for example, a speaker may say:

Téann Máire ar scoil.	Goes Mary to school.
Tá Máire ag dul ar scoil.	Be Mary at go to school.
Bíonn Máire ag dul ar scoil.	Be + habitual Mary at go to school.

thus adding a nuance to the distinction made in English.

Irish speakers, used to such fine distinctions, expected their English to provide similar nuances, and indeed speakers of Hiberno-English added an extra feature of differentiation in that they can say:

Mary goes to school.
Mary is going to school.
Mary biz/bees going to school
Mary does be going to school.

The third sentence suggests regularity and the fourth both regularity and habitualness.

When we try to explain a grammatical distinction in a language that does not make such a distinction, we face certain difficulties. We can either make the original speakers sound funny or stupid or very unusual. Yet the distinctions we have illustrated were, and are, as significant to Gaelic speakers as the distinction between 'can' and 'could' might be for a speaker of English. Perhaps the simplest way to illustrate the nuance of difference between 'biz' and 'does be' is to take an example from live speech. Female A was house-proud and liked her drying cloth to be on its peg when not in use. Female B often left the drying cloth on the draining board and was told: '*That cloth biz on the peg when it doesn't be drying dishes!*'

Interestingly, when President Clinton gave testimony on video in August 1998, he drew attention to the ambiguity of 'is'. If a person says: 'He is not sleeping with X' it can mean 'He is not sleeping with X at this precise moment' or 'He does not sleep with X'. The distinction he made was linguistically correct, although many speakers of English failed to see it. Hiberno-English could have helped to illustrate the nuance he was trying to highlight!

It is now taken for granted that English speakers can use structures like:

> *He's reading a book.*
> *She's planning to run a half marathon.*
> *The kettle is boiling.*

However, such constructions are not a feature of Germanic or Romance languages and, although Old English developed the ability to use 'progressive structures', the development does not seem to have occurred in other Germanic dialects. Barbara Strang says:

> *... we find in 970 two tenses, past and non-past...*

> (*A History of English*, 1974: 305)

and she even uses the metaphor of 'grafting' to draw attention to the fact that:

> *English is most remarkable for the grafting on to its historical two-tense inflectional verb-system of an elaborate network of modal, aspectual and clause-contrastive systems ...*

> (*A History of English*, 1970: 98)

It would be interesting to pursue the question of why English, alone of the languages spoken by Anglo-Saxons, Latin-using clerics, Vikings and Norman French, makes a grammatical distinction that is unusual in those languages but is a marked feature of the Celtic tongues. Could it be that English speakers borrowed such a distinction from the Celts, who previously lived throughout Ireland and Britain? Many traditional linguists would be appalled at the suggestion. After all, it has become a truism of descriptions of English to comment on the slightness of the Celtic influence on English. W. Nelson Francis's account is reasonably typical:

> *... except for geographical names like* Avon *and* Carlisle *and topographical terms like* down *(n. 'low hill') and* tor, *few Celtic words came into English at this time.*

> (*The English Language*, 1974: 145)

It seems highly improbable that such a claim as Francis's could be true. However, even if the Celts only contributed a few words to Old English, the likelihood is that their later influence on the language has been overlooked and underestimated by scholars who did not know – or perhaps did not even want to know – the Celtic languages. Again, a useful analogy is African-American English. When some non-African commentators examined African-American English, they saw it as 'a debased dialect'. When scholars with a knowledge of African languages examined it, however, they discovered that African influences permeated African-American English, and that these influences were in no way limited simply to the vocabulary.

There is an Irish Gaelic proverb that has been quoted many times. It says:

Is buaine port ná glór na n-éan.	A melody is more durable than the song of a bird.
Is buaine focal ná toice an tsaoghail.	A word is more durable than the wealth of the world

The proverb suggests that it is *what* we create that endures. The Gaelic musicians and poets may have died, but their melodies and their ideas have lived on. They have survived in the folk traditions of the people and they have been carried around the world, not in Gaelic but in English.

Writers who comment on the lack of Celtic influence on English would find a rich seam in the language associated with religion. The English word *dock*, for example, has an uncertain history and English etymologists have been known to suggest an onomatopoeic origin rather than to refer to Breton *kloc'h*, Cornish *doch*, Irish *doc, dog* or Welsh *doch*. And yet, the use of the bell, which ultimately gave rise to the striking clock, in church ceremonies was virtually unknown in Roman-oriented worship. Describing the unexpected similarities between the early Coptic and Celtic churches, William Dalrymple (1998: 419) says:

> *The handbell played a very prominent place in ritual, so much so that in early Irish sculpture clerics are distinguished from lay persons by placing a clochette in their hand ... yet bells of any sort are quite unknown in the dominant Greek or Latin Churches until the tenth century at the earliest.*

CHAPTER FIVE

The Spread of Green English

I met another notable man in the last year of my Cameroons period, a
purser of one of the Elder Dempster ships, Roger Casement ... he spent his
time hunting for plants and rare flowers ... He made several voyages
when I was at Bethel ... We all loved him and were never happier than
when we had Casement as our guest.

(T. Lewis, *These Seventy Years*, n.d: 88)

So far, most comments have been restricted to Ireland and Britain,
but Irish English has spread far beyond these islands. Because of the
Irish diaspora, elements of Green English have been carried from Belfast to Boston, Galway to the Gambia and Tipperary to Tasmania.

**It would be out of place here to discuss in detail the similarities
between Irish and American English, but a few pointers may
be of interest:**

BBC English	Gen. American English	Irish English
22 vowel sounds	16 vowel sounds	16 vowel sounds
24 consonants	25 consonants	26 consonants
non-rhotic	rhotic	rhotic
face flannel	washcloth	facecloth
spanner	monkey wrench	wrench/spanner
she is allowed to do it	she gets to do it	she gets doing it
she would have gone if she had been asked	she would have gone if she would have been asked	she would have gone if she would have been asked

**It could be argued that some of the above features were
probably current in seventeenth-century England, too. For a
variety of reasons, however, American English and Irish
English have developed and retained characteristics not found
in England.**

It is hard to be precise about when Irish-influenced English began to be carried abroad. If we think back to the christianising of England and Scotland from the fifth century onwards, we could list generations of Irish saints who lived and worked throughout Europe. It is not possible to say what language these Irish missionaries used, although it seems likely that they would have preached to ordinary people in the language of the ordinary people.

> In 635, King Oswald of Northumbria asked for Irish missionaries to be sent to evangelise his kingdom. The first missionary sent from Iona gave up, claiming that the Northumbrians were so stubborn that he could make no headway with them! Aidan suggested that all groups could be educated and redeemed and he was sent as bishop to be a missionary to Oswald's people.

That might, initially, suggest that they occasionally used Old English or Old Scots, but it is also possible that they preached to their Celtic-using cousins mainly in a Celtic language. After all, parts of England such as Cornwall remained Celtic speaking until the recent past. The links between the early churches in Brittany, Cornwall, Ireland, the Isle of Man, the north of England and Scotland can be illustrated by their shared respect for such Irish names as *Ronan* (a name that means 'little seal' and invokes a tradition that predates Christianity).

> Ronan comes from Irish *rón*, 'a seal', and means 'little seal'. It is found as a first name in Brittany and Scotland, as well as Ireland. According to tradition, mermaids could take on the form of a seal. If a man found the seal's skin when the mermaid was not in it, she could be persuaded to live with him as his wife. Their children were then 'ronans' or 'little seals'.

Early manuscripts

It is likely, however, that some of the missionaries spoke Old English. It is certainly true that the Irish monks who worked on illuminated manuscripts influenced the shape of the letters that were used to write Old English. Admittedly, the Irish alphabet was based on the Latin one, but Irish modifications were transferred to Old English. For example, the letter 'ð' was borrowed to represent the initial sound of words like 'the' and 'than'. It is even possible that a knowledge of Irish orthographic conventions may shed light on the very first Christian poem ever composed in English. The poem is usually referred to as Caedmon's Hymn and an eighth-century version begins:

Nu scylon her ʒan	*hefaen-ricaes uard*
(Now [we] must praise	[of] heaven kingdom [the] guardian)
metudaes maecti	*end his mod-ʒidanc*
([the] Maker's powers	and his mind-thought)
uerc uuldur-fadur	*sue he uundra ʒihuaes*
([the] works of glory-father	as he of wonders each)
eci dryctin	*or astelidae*
(eternal Lord	[the] beginning established)

Caedmon's name is partly Celtic and is similar in structure and meaning to *Cadoc*, 'brave in battle', *Caderyn*, 'lord of battle', and *Cathal*, 'powerful in battle'. According to a tradition beginning with Bede, Caedmon was a swineherd at the Christian monastic settlement of Whitby. This settlement had strong cultural links with Ireland. St Aidan, who died in 651, was said to have taken Christianity there, and the struggle between Irish Christianity and Roman Christianity was settled at the Synod of Whitby in 663. Caedmon's poem was written between 657 and 680 and he is the first to use pagan poetic traditions to celebrate the glory of the Christian God.

> **Barbara Strang describes the Old English poetic structure as follows:**
> *The unit of the verse is a two-part line; there is no higher structural unit ... A major structural break within the line, which we may call the caesura, divides it into two parts, which in principle are the same in structure, but which are subtly differentiated ... The half-lines are linked in pairs by initial rhyme or alliteration. Alliteration depends on likeness of initial sound – normally membership of the same phoneme, but ... all vowels alliterate together.*
> (*A History of English*, 1974: 324)

In traditional Old English poetry, half-lines were linked by alliteration, usually in a pattern of two alliterating words in the first half-line and one in the second. We get this in lines 2 and 3 and in 4, in that all vowels were held to alliterate:

m	m	m	
w	w	w	
e		o	a

It is a surprise, therefore, that the very first line breaks the rules in that we have:

n	h	h

If, however, we remember that Irish 'n' and Irish 'h' differed only in the fact that the 'h' had an ascender:

ꝯ ꞃ

and if we hypothesise that the scribe wrote 'h' not 'n', then we would have the correct alliterative pattern:

h	h	h

and the meaning would change from:

Now we must praise the Guardian of the heavenly kingdom

to:

How must we praise the Guardian of the heavenly kingdom.

The lack of punctuation marks in Old English poetry would not rule out a question. Caedmon, like all those associated with monastic settlements, would have known that several of the psalms begin with questions, including psalms that were frequently used for monastic meditations such as 'How long wilt thou forget me, O Lord?' and 'My God, my God, why hast thou forsaken me?'

> *In the sixth century the Celtic Church in Ireland was a centre of remarkable missionary activity. Irish missionaries moved relentlessly up the western coasts of Scotland, founding centres like Iona and Applecross ... But in addition to organized missionary expeditions, Irish anchorites were quartering the northern seas in their frail curraghs in search of empty islands where they could cultivate solitude, and shortly after 700 they reached the then uninhabited Faroes ...*
>
> (Magnus Magnusson and Hermann Pålsson,
> *The Vinland Sagas*, 1965: 13)

The Americas

The Irish were early visitors to the Americas, too. St Brendan the Navigator (484–577) is thought to have visited the continent in the sixth century. This was four centuries before Leif Eriksson, the Norse navigator, island-hopped in 996 from Norway via Iceland to Greenland and 'Vinland', now believed to be the coastal area of north-east America. Eriksson's journey is of significance in this narrative because he took an Irish man and woman with him and released them on the American coast to see if the land was habitable. This is how the medieval saga writer describes the incident:

> *When the ship had passed Furdustrands* [possibly the Gulf of St Lawrence] *the two Scots were put ashore and told to run southwards to explore the country's resources, and to return within three days. They each wore a garment called a bjafal, which had a hood at the top and was open at the sides; it had no sleeves and was fastened between the legs with a loop and a button. That was all they wore.*
>
> *The ship cast anchor there and waited, and after three days the Scots came running down the shore; one of them was carrying some grapes, and the other some wild wheat. They told Karlsefni that they thought they had found good land.*
>
> (Magnusson and Pålsson, *The Vinland Sagas*, 1965: 95)

The term 'Scot' was the usual one applied to someone from the north of Ireland. The name of the garment they wore might have been as close as the Vikings could get to the pronunciation of Gaelic *cabhail*, 'a sleeveless shirt', or *giobhail*, 'a garment'. The runners were not speakers of English but would almost certainly have spoken and understood Old Norse, as would many of the Irish during the ninth, tenth and eleventh centuries.

The references so far are all part of folklore, although modern historians recognise both the value and the accuracy of oral traditions. We know that Irish people travelled throughout the known world but we cannot be certain what language they spoke outside Ireland.

The Irish in England

We might suggest that when speakers of Middle English adopted the word 'kern' (from Irish *ceithern*, for 'a band of foot soldiers'), it probably meant that they had Irish soldiers as well as the name in their armies. We can, however, be absolutely certain of Irish people travelling abroad and speaking a form of English from the beginning of the seventeenth century. As the Plantation of Ireland was taking place, many Irish people, deprived of their land and their livelihood, returned the compliment and settled in London. The Privy Council did not receive these visitors with much warmth and wrote accordingly to Lord Chichester, the Lord Deputy of Ireland:

> *You shall understand that these parts of London and elsewhere are exceedingly pestered with a great multitude of beggars of that country [Ireland] ... most of them peasants with wives and children, the disorder whereof must needs proceed by the negligence of the officers of ports and the owners of barks, for which we pray you to take better order and severely to punish all offenders; considering how great a dishonour it is that strangers should behold them in our highways and streets, and a great eyesore it is to his majesty's poor subjects in this kingdom.*

The Irish were not the only immigrants that England would have preferred not to have. Africans and people of African origin were also unwelcome, as a proclamation towards the end of Elizabeth I's reign makes clear:

There are of late divers blackmoores brought into this realme, of which kinde of people there are already here to manie ... Her Majesty's pleasure therefore ys that those kind of people should be sent forthe of the lande ...

In spite of the hostile reception that many of the Irish received, they continued to find their way to England. In 1753, the London magistrate Saunders Welsh, in a classic response to outsiders, whether Irish, Gypsy or Black, divided the Irish in Britain into two classes: those who were poor but industrious and thrifty and:

The others are a set of fellows made desperate by their crimes, and whose stay in Ireland being no longer safe, come to London to perpetuate their outrages, and it may be justly asserted that most of the robberies, and the murders consequent upon them, have been committed by these outcasts from Ireland.

It would not have been possible for 'most of the robberies' to have been committed by Irish people unless, of course, highwaymen like Dick Turpin (1706–39) should be referred to as Declan O'Turpin. However, the quotation illustrates three points: large numbers of Irish were already living in England in the eighteenth century; for the most part, they lived in poverty; there was widespread prejudice against them. The poverty in which many of the Irish emigrants lived in England throughout the seventeenth, eighteenth and nineteenth centuries was such that, in 1817:

... it was estimated that nineteen out of twenty persons receiving relief [in St Giles, London] *were Irish.*
(M.D. George, *London Life in the Eighteenth Century*, 1966: 129)

Nor was London the only city where the Irish were found in sufficiently large numbers to influence patterns of speech. According to George:

The pressure of the Irish poor threatened to break down the poor law machinery in some of the London parishes as well as in Liverpool and Manchester.
(M.D. George, *London Life in the Eighteenth Century*, 1966: 121)

As with most of these references, little attempt is made to comment on language matters, although Montague Gore in 1851 told his readers about an influx of people fleeing from the Great Hunger in Ireland. He describes:

> *Squalid children, haggard men, with long uncombed hair, in rags, with a short pipe in their mouths, many speaking Irish,* [and, by implication, many others speaking a form of English] *women without shoes or stockings ...*

Living in such conditions, it would be surprising if some of the men had not turned to burglary or the women to prostitution. That the Irish were thus in a position to intersperse some Gaelic words and idioms into criminal cant (perhaps from Irish *cainnt*, 'talk') is hardly disputable. And one of the side effects of their method of making a living is that some of the Irish could also be transported to the colonies as enforced labourers.

The world-wide use of *boycott*, meaning 'embargo', 'withdraw co-operation', 'strike', had its origins in Ireland. Charles Cunningham Boycott (1832–97) was a land agent in Mayo. He would not implement the reforms suggested by the Irish Land League (1879–81), but was forced to give in when his tenants refused to work for him.

The Irish in the colonies

The influence of Irish English was not, of course, limited to Britain. Richard Hakluyt (?1552–1616) lists the type of settler needed in the colonies. He includes carpenters, millwrights and joiners, gardeners, especially those who could cultivate vines and olives, builders and soldiers for the protection of colonists. Because such people were not initially eager to travel, Hakluyt was also willing to consider men who had lost their money and self respect, imprisoned debtors, ex-soldiers and children of wandering beggars. Many Irish people, especially those who had been driven off their land to make room for the British planters, certainly fell into this latter category.

It is advisable not to assume that all comments on the Irish in Britain in the nineteenth century are either accurate or just. The *Punch* caricature of the Irishman as Frankenstein's Monster underlines the mistrust in which many of the Irish were held.

' THE IRISH FRANKENSTEIN.

Reference to Irish people travelling to the Americas go back, as we have seen, to the mythical voyages of St Brendan and the historical journeys of Leif Eriksson. They went in much greater numbers, however, from the middle of the seventeenth century. Cromwell's cruel treatment of the Irish is well-known, in Ireland at least.

It would be wrong to think that Cromwell's 'justice' was levelled against the Irish alone. He expected his soldiers to behave with courage and honour. To encourage good behaviour among them, he had rules about the treatment of the women who were known as 'camp followers': English women were whipped and sent away; Scottish women had their nose and ears cut off; and Irish women were executed.

What is less well-known is his connection with the West Indies. His forces, for example, seized Jamaica from the Spanish in 1655 and defeated the Spanish West India fleet off Santa Cruz in 1657. He also continued a policy begun by Elizabeth of transporting Irish 'trouble-makers' to the colonies.

Early English immigrants to Jamaica found the climate hard and so, on September 26, 1655, a committee of the Council of State agreed that 1,000 Irish girls and 1,000 Irish youths of fourteen years and under were to be sent to Jamaica.

From the middle of the seventeenth century, we find sporadic references to the Irish, especially in Barbados, Monserrat and St Kitts. A Jesuit priest who visited Barbados as early as 1643 wrote that there were a few Catholics on the island 'both English and Irish'. In September, 1649, Cromwell wrote to the Speaker of the House of Commons from Dublin to report that Drogheda had been overcome:

> *When they submitted, their officers were knocked on the head; and every tenth man of the soldiers killed; and the rest shipped for the Barbadoes. The soldiers in the other Tower were all spared, as to their lives only; and shipped likewise for the Barbadoes.*
> (Thomas Carlyle, *Oliver Cromwell's Letters and Speeches*, Part V, Letter CV)

Most were transported as indentured labourers and treated as harshly as the African slaves. In certain cases, slaves were treated better because they cost money whereas indentured labourers could be replaced free. The Irish were not always well liked by their British 'masters', who criticised them for being lazy and for being too friendly with the African slaves. Indeed, in 1657 an Order was issued in Barbados stating that the Irish – both free men and servants – should be considered dangerous and be disarmed. This was, in part, due to the fact that the Irish were Catholic and had a history of refusing to fight against the French or the Spanish. In the 1640s, for example, the Irish in St Kitts moved to the neighbouring island of Saba to avoid fighting against England's enemies. Precise figures are hard to come by. However, it seems likely that the Irish were the second largest English-speaking group in the Caribbean in the seventeenth century. The descendants of these so-called 'redlegs' or 'black Irish' are found on several of the Caribbean islands.

> *Notwithstanding Barbados hath beene soe magnifyed for her strength, I find not above 4,000 ffighting men uppon the Place; here are 2,000 Irish, I wish I had soe many Scots for them ...*
> (letter dated, 7 May, 1667, Harlow, *History of Barbados 1625-85*)

We do not know what language or languages the transported Irish spoke. The fact that there is a valley in Monserrat called Glenmor (Gaelic *gleann mór*, 'big glen') suggests that some of the Irish may well have spoken Gaelic. John Wells (*Accents of English*, 1982: 586) notes that:

> *Monserrat itself was probably first settled in 1633, by a group of disaffected Irish Catholics from the nearby St Kitts*

and an Irish priest who visited Monserrat in 1643 claimed that English, French and Irish were:

> *used freely in this part of the world.*

But Irish Gaelic would have been of little use as a lingua franca, especially since many of the Irish intermarried with the Africans. Today's families of Christies, Fitzgeralds, Rileys, Ryans, Murphys and Sweeneys speak Caribbean English and it seems likely that Irish men and African women would have used a form of English as their home language. The Irish were thus in a position to influence Caribbean

English from the earliest days of English colonisation, and many Caribbean linguists have drawn attention to rhythmic and structural similarities between Irish and Caribbean speech. They both have a tendency to prefer *dis* and *dat* to 'this' and 'that'. They can both refer to a child being *old-fashioned* and mean 'smart beyond their years' and they can both combine 'do' and 'be' as in:

He does be comin'.

Indeed, a Guyanese linguist told me about going into a pub in London and turning to speak to a 'Jamaican' who turned out to be a Kerry man!

But the Irish also went to both North and South America. By 1685, there were indentured Irish labourers in all thirteen of the English colonies. By the 1690s, there were so many in Maryland, South Carolina and Virginia that laws were passed limiting their immigration, even as servants. A hundred years later, Irish soldiers fought on both sides of the American War of Independence and their courage was acknowledged by both American and British generals. By the 1790s, the three most numerous anglophone groups in the United States were the English, the Irish and the African-Americans. It seems probable that, at this time, there were over one third of a million Irish in the United States, a figure that was considerably augmented after the failed 1798 Rebellion in Ireland. This uprising saw Catholics and Non-Conformists uniting to fight for an independent country. When it failed, thousands of Ulster Non-Conformists joined the exodus of Catholics to avoid the draconian Penal Code against both denominations. The migration gave rise to the American classification 'Scotch-Irish', an attempt to label Ulster people by their speech, which was similar to Scots and Irish but identical to neither. Many of the 'Scotch-Irish' settled in Pennsylvania, the Carolinas, in Georgia, Alabama and Virginia. Scholars have drawn attention to the similarities between Irish and Appalachian folk culture, especially the music. It was not only fiddles and melodies that these Irish emigrants carried to the United States. They took some of their sounds, their words and idioms. These have left their mark on American speech. Many speakers in the USA, for example, rhyme 'not' and 'sat', 'join' and 'wine', and in Northern Ireland, even today, a child called Nat(haniel) Brown is teased: 'If you're not Brown, who are you?' The question would be meaningful in many parts of America but not in England.

The Irish in America

That the Irish were in America in sufficient numbers to influence speech patterns during the seventeenth and eighteenth centuries is beyond dispute. The potential impact became much greater during the second half of the nineteenth century, however, when perhaps as many as four and a half million Irish people sailed to Ellis Island and the hope of a new life. The emigration continued during the twentieth century and today an estimated one in four people in the United States claims Irish ancestry. The figures are not in contention, but did the Irish influence American English? The answer has to be a categoric 'yes'. Anyone who has listened to the two varieties has noticed similarities in sound and rhythm. As far as words are concerned, the Irish are likely to have contributed to the use of 'youse' as a plural of 'you' and possibly to the slang word *kibosh*, in that this could be from *cap* + *báis*, 'death cap'. This might help explain the idiom 'put the kibosh on something'. Other borrowings from Irish English may include such well-known items as *shanty*, *shenanigans*, *slogan* and *suggans*, as well as perhaps one of the best-known phrases in the language. 'So long' is made up of English words but neither has really anything to do with 'goodbye'. The Irish word *slán* literally means 'safety' but was and is used when people are parting:

Slán leat   (= may safety go with thee)
Slán agat   (= may safety stay with thee).

US word	Meaning	Irish Gaelic	Meaning
buns	bottom	bun	base, bottom

US word	Meaning	Irish Gaelic	Meaning
ballyhoo	commotion	bailiú (daoine)	gathering of people
bonnyclabber	thick sour milk	bainne clabair	curds
cop	seize, understand	ceap	seize, think
hobo	outcast	ob	reject, shun
slogan	motto	slua gairm	warriors' call
slug	mouthful	slog	gulp, swallow
shanty	poor dwelling	sean teach	shack

The Irish in Canada

Canada, too, took its share of Irish emigrants. In addition, its speech patterns are increasingly similar to those of its powerful neighbour. Irish speakers were in parts of Canada from the early sixteenth century and may have contributed one particular linguistic feature, namely the tendency to use what is called a 'narrative *eh*' as in:

> *Are you listening, eh? Well, those shoes I bought, eh, are the most uncomfortable I've ever worn, eh. They hurt everywhere, eh, at my toes, eh, and my heels ...*

The tag used in Ireland can vary from 'eh' to 'ah' but it is sufficiently similar to suggest a link. The majority of Irish settlers in Canada were from the North of Ireland. Their influence tended to blend with the Scots, both English and Gaelic-speaking, who were there in sufficient numbers to warrant the naming of a state Nova Scotia, 'New Scotland'.

The Irish in Australia

According to most history books, Captain James Cook (1728–79) sailed down the west coast of Australia and, in 1770, claimed this large southern continent for Britain. He paid scant attention to the facts that the continent had already been named New Holland by earlier European explorers, or that there were already hundreds of thousands of Aborigine dwellers, who were seldom consulted about names. By 1787, Britain had lost the United States and had to find new penal colonies for its convicts. It chose Botany Bay in Australia, a name that many would like to see replaced by 'Gillingarie', which comes from the Dharawal language and means 'land that belongs to us all'.

It is perhaps worth reminding ourselves that many of the 'convicts' were simply destitute people, who were jailed for stealing food, or were women or girls who could not support themselves. By 1798, Irish rebels were being sent to Australia and many others chose to go there willingly, especially in the nineteenth century when Australia's rich gold mines began to be exploited. It is this time that is described in countless Irish songs, such as 'The Wild Colonial Boy':

> *He robbed the rich to feed the poor;*
> *All arms he did destroy.*
> *A terror to Australia was*
> *The wild colonial boy.*

and most people have heard of the legendary Ned Kelly (1855–80), whose last thoughts before he was hanged appear to have been about England's exploitation of the Irish:

> *... many a blooming Irishman rather than subdue to the Saxon yoke were flogged to death and bravely died ...*

The Irish probably shared 'youse' with Australia as well as the name 'Sheila', which became a colloquial equivalent of 'woman':

> *She's a real fine sheila.*

And, they may also have provided Australia with such words as *bar* as in 'I haven't heard a bar all day'; *barrack*, 'to support strongly'; *dag* for an unattractive person; as well as items like *blarney*, a word which has been popularised worldwide.

At the level of the sentence, it is possible that the Australianism:

> *She's wrapped in him.*   (= she's very much in love with him)

is derived from:

> *Tá sí dúnta i ngrá leis.*   (= she's enclosed in love for him)

and we shall limit our comments to two further structures. Many Australians, like the Irish, will say, for example:

It serves him right. (even, occasionally, *It deserves him right.*)

It does not.

It does so, (so it does).

Most English speakers would simply say:

It does.

and Americans would prefer:

It does too.

In addition, they often use 'must not' where an English speaker would prefer 'cannot':

Australian/Irish:	*You mustn't have told him!*
English:	*You can't have told him!*

One of the most contentious issues in Australian usage is the pronunciation of the letter 'h'. The *Sydney Morning Herald* **(5 November, 1997: 26) wrote:**

> *This column does not want to seem snobbish, and God knows, we have nothing against people who went through the Catholic school system but yesterday we happened to hear an interview ... Clark referred to the exam as the 'aitch ess see' and Niland referred to it as the 'haitch ess see' ... this column ... can't help wondering how any person who pronounces aitch as haitch can presume to comment on the educational standards of this State...*

Frederick Ludowyk writes about how Irish immigrants may have carried 'haitch' with them (*Ozwords***, Vol. 4.1, 1988: 3).**

> *If the dropping of aitch is a social marker, the pronunciation of the letter 'h' can also be a social, political, and sectarian marker. In the Irish Republic, the 'haitch' pronunciation is common, but the situation is more complex in Northern Ireland where, it is claimed, Catholics say 'haitch', whereas the royalist Protestants say 'aitch'.*

My favourite claim in the article is:

> *The received wisdom is that 'haitch' was introduced to Australia by Irish Sisters of Mercy and Irish Christian Brothers teaching in their Irish Australian schools. But today, even in the absence of linguistically subversive Irish nuns, Australians continue to 'haitch'.*

The Irish in New Zealand

New Zealand also attracted Irish settlers, mostly during the last one hundred years. More were from Ulster than from the other provinces. The Ulster Scots influence blended with that of the Scots, who settled especially in the South Island, as the placenames *Ben Nevis*, *Dunedin*, *Invercargill* and *Stewart Island* attest. Such words as *skite*, 'splash', and *whinge*, 'complain in a whining way', may come from either Scots or Ulster Scots. The New Zealand use of 'whenever' rather than 'when' as in:

> *Whenever we were children, there was no television.*

is found mainly in Northern Ireland, and suggests an influence that has often been overlooked.

The Irish in Africa and Asia

Africa and Asia are the two remaining continents and they, too, share some linguistic features with Ireland. We do not know exactly when the Irish first travelled to Africa or Asia. Unlike most west European nations, the Irish did not pursue a policy of colonisation, largely because they were so busy fending off colonisers themselves! Often, however, we can find unexpected references, as in the following account of a journey made by Thomas Phillips near the source of the River Gambia in 1693:

> *The next to him was Mr William Ronan, an Irish gentleman, who had lived long in France, and spake the language fluently, as well as the bastard Portuguese the negroes use along this coast.*

The narrative does not tell us how on earth William Ronan managed to make his way to the Gambia or what he was doing there. Did he spend the rest of his life there? Did he have children whose descendants are still in the Gambia? We have no way of knowing. Writers like Thomas Phillips tell us what interested them, not what a modern reader might want to know.

The Irish in the army

A brief foray into history provides clear information on the role of Irish soldiers around the world. They were to be found – sometimes on both sides! – in such major conflicts as the Hundred Years War (1337–1453), the Wars of the Roses (1455–85), the Civil War in England (1642–48), the Thirty Years War (1618–48), the War of the Spanish Succession (1701–14), the War of the Polish Succession (1730–38), the War of the Austrian Succession (1740–48), the Seven Years War (1756–63), the American War of Independence (1775–83), the Napoleonic Wars (1799–1815), the Mexican-American War (1846–48), the Crimean War (1853–56), the American Civil War (1861–65), the Boer War (1899–1902), the First World War (1914–18), the Spanish Civil War (1936–39), the Second World War (1939–45), the Falklands War (1982), the Gulf War (1991), and they were well represented in the wars of Independence in South America. In this context, Ambrosio O'Higgins (1720–1801) warrants a mention, in that he became Viceroy of Chile (1789–96) and of Peru (1796–1801). His son, Bernardo (1778–1842), fought for Chile against Spain and became Chile's first President in 1817.

The Irish in the professions

The Irish have been soldiers in other peoples' wars at least as far back as the fourteenth century, but they have been even more influential as teachers and missionaries, journalists and broadcasters. Between 1870 and 1970, Ireland produced more missionaries for a country of its population than any other country on earth. These missionaries founded schools in Argentina and Australia, Bolivia and Botswana, Cameroon and China, Ghana and Guyana, India and Irian Jaya, Nigeria and Nepal, Pakistan and Papua New Guinea, Singapore and Sri Lanka, Tahiti and Tanzania, and many other countries as well. In each of these areas, Irish teachers have taught English and spread the love of talking as an art form as well as an admiration for good communicators, whether in speech or in writing. As well as the standard language, they have also shored up such Irish features as the (mis)pronunciation of 'grievous' and 'mischievous' as 'grievious' and 'mischievious', and an un-English use of 'bring' and 'take' as in:

Bring those books to my office and wait for me there.

and such idioms as:

cook the fish in its shape = cook the fish whole; don't cut it up
sing your heart out = sing as well and as enthusiastically as possible
sit your ground = stay where you are
take the floor = get up and dance

Irish models in the pulpit, the hospital, and the school have influenced local norms of educated speech in virtually every country to which the English language has been carried.

> **A competition run by the SABC in the 1960s to find 'The Voice of South Africa' was won by an Irishman, Paddy O'Byrne.**

This chapter has moved out of Ireland and surveyed the spread of aspects of Green English from Ireland to North America, the Caribbean, Africa, Asia and Australia. Ireland was used by Raleigh as a testing ground for fortress design, and for trying out the potato and tobacco. Partly as a consequence of such actions, Irish speakers helped in the formation of Colonial Englishes from the sixteenth century onwards. And from those beginnings, an essential part of today's World English has a green hue – how green is still to be determined!

There is an interesting footnote that might be added to this chapter. On 6 December 1492, Columbus landed on the island of Quisqueya, which he called Hispaniola. In their account of this momentous event, Luis de Torres and Rodrigo de Jerez make the first references to smoking tobacco and the term they use is of interest. They report seeing Caribs who 'drink smoke'. Now we know that Sir Walter Raleigh subsequently introduced tobacco smoking into Ireland and England. In English, the expression used was simply 'smoking' but, in Irish, the expression used was *ag ól tabac*, 'drinking tobacco', a close translation from the original Carib. It is known that Sir Walter was accompanied on his voyages of discovery by Irishmen, some of whom probably survived and returned home. Raleigh himself was imprisoned by James I in 1603. One year later, James wrote his *Counterblaste to Tobacco*, in which he described smoking as:

> *a custom lothsome to the eye, hatefull to the nose, harmefull to the braine, dangerous to the lungs.*

CHAPTER SIX

From Runes to Roddy Doyle

'O Finn, what is the best music in the world?'
'The best music in the world is the music of what happens.'

Traditional wisdom

There has been an unbroken tradition of Irish literature from about the sixth century. However, orature in Ireland must go back to the first time Irish people had the leisure to sit round a fire and weave a narrative or sing a song. The earliest written records are runic, but runes were carved, usually on wood, and thus few have survived. Those that have lasted suggest that the runes were associated with magic and the supernatural, a link that is easy to understand. Think of how members of a non-literate society might have felt if they saw someone read a message from a few carved lines! They must have felt something of the awe that the people in Oliver Goldsmith's village felt for their parson:

> *Amazed the gazing rustics rang'd around,*
> *And still they gaz'd, and still the wonder grew*
> *That one small head could carry all he knew.*

('The Deserted Village')

The Irish tradition of literature written in English can be traced to the fourteenth century, and it has continued to flower, so that in the twentieth century no fewer that four Nobel laureates were Irish writers of English.

WINNERS OF THE NOBEL PRIZE FOR LITERATURE FOR IRELAND,
THE UNITED KINGDOM AND THE UNITED STATES

Ireland	UK	USA
W.B.Yeats, 1923	R. Kipling, 1907	S. Lewis, 1930
G.B. Shaw, 1927	J. Galsworthy, 1932	E. O'Neill, 1936
S. Beckett, 1969	T.S. Eliot, 1948	Pearl Buck, 1938
S. Heaney, 1995	B. Russell, 1950	W. Faulkner, 1949
	W. Churchill, 1953	E. Hemingway, 1954
	W. Golding, 1983	J. Steinbeck, 1962
		S. Bellow, 1976
		Toni Morrison, 1993

For its population, Ireland has been honoured more for literature in English than either the UK or the USA. In addition, one might well ask why James Joyce is missing from the list. He is currently offered for study in every English Literature department in British universities, whereas Nobel laureates Lewis, Russell and Churchill do not seem to feature. The award of the Nobel Prize for literature does not, of course, guarantee the quality of the writers, but whatever criteria are applied, Irish writers of literature in English are recognised as among the best in the world. Viewed objectively, this is an extraordinary phenomenon, and one that is worthy of serious consideration.

> *Who killed James Joyce?*
> *I, said the commentator,*
> *I killed James Joyce*
> *For my graduation.*
>
> *What weapon was used*
> *To slay mighty Ulysses?*
> *The weapon that was used*
> *Was a Harvard thesis.*
>
> (Patrick Kavanagh)

In the Middle Ages, 'originality' meant 'having existed from the beginning' and so the literature that was prized as 'original' was likely to be 'what oft was thought but ne'er so well expressed'. Often, the name of the writer of a piece of great literature is unknown. By the time of the second wave of English influence in Ireland, 'original' was taking on its modern meaning of 'innovative'. It is from this period, from the early seventeenth century onwards, that individual Irish writers come into view.

Writings in Anglo-Irish, that is, in the language of people whose ancestral mother tongue was English but who were born and brought up in Ireland, have been admired throughout the English-speaking world. One of the earliest of these was **James Ussher** (1581–1656), who became the Archbishop of Armagh. He was renowned in his day for the balance and wisdom of his writing, although he is remembered today, if at all, because of his acceptance of the literal truth of the Bible. He calculated that the world was created by God, 4004 years before the birth of Christ (probably in the morning of 4 September).

James Ussher was born in Dublin in 1581, when Elizabeth I was on the throne, and died in 1656, when England was a Republic. He was ordained an Anglican priest in 1601 and became chancellor of St Patrick's Cathedral two years later. In 1607, he became Professor of Divinity at Trinity College and held the post until 1620. He left the academic life to become Bishop of Meath in 1620 and in 1625 he became Archbishop of Armagh. Ussher went to England in 1640 and, when his Irish estates were confiscated, he remained there working on his major work, *Annals of the World*. These were written in Latin and translated into English two years after his death. In his *Annals*, he worked out the chronology of the Bible, claiming that the Creation had occurred 4004 years before the birth of Christ. Ussher's chronology was accepted by most scholars and Christians and included in King James's Authorised Version, published in 1611.

Anglo-Irish writers

From the late seventeenth century onwards, Anglo-Irish dramatists were well represented in the British theatre. Simply by mentioning **Susannah Centlivre** (1670–1723), **Richard Steele** (1672–1729),

George Farquhar (1678–1707), **Oliver Goldsmith** (1728–74), **Richard Brinsley Sheridan** (1751–1816), **Oscar Wilde** (1854–1900), **George Bernard Shaw** (1856–1950) and **Samuel Beckett** (1906–89), we are listing some of the best-known dramatists in the language, dramatists whose works continue to be performed and studied. Some critics, of course, forget that they are Irish, and some have insisted that:

> ... *there is nothing of Ireland in them*
> (A.E. Malone, *The Irish Drama 1896–1928*, 1929: 15)

and yet, when Malone attempts to characterise Irish dramatists, we see the qualities he highlights in the works of all the Anglo-Irish playwrights listed above. According to Malone (p. 15), the defining quality of Irish drama is:

> ... *a perfection of dialogue which is quite distinctively Irish; and they all have wit which is no less a distinguishing mark of the Irishman* [Most critics would certainly want to add 'and woman'].

and he goes on:

> *Comedies by English writers tend to be humorous and sentimental, while comedies by Irishmen tend to be witty and ironic.*

Nor is Malone the only critic to comment on the linguistic felicities of writers who grew up using a form of Green English. D.E.S. Maxwell (*A Critical History of Modern Irish Drama*, 1984: 2) attributes the success of Irish dramatists to:

> ... *a peculiarly but not uniquely Irish acknowledgement of the sovereignty of words.*

Maxwell is, of course, right to point out that the 'gift of the gab' is not limited to the Irish. However, it is interesting how often literature in English flourishes when there is another language in the background. It is surely not a coincidence that the Nobel laureates for literature in English since 1991 include Nadine Gordimer from multilingual South Africa, Derek Walcott from bilingual St Lucia, Toni Morrison, who insists on the African element in her American writing, and Seamus Heaney from Ireland.

Pre-eminent though Anglo-Irish writers were in drama, they were also well represented in prose and poetry. Richard Steele was not only a dramatist, but a journalist who was instrumental in the success of both *The Tatler* and *The Spectator*. It would be hard to overstate the significance of these journals in the establishment of eighteenth-century English opinion. The two other writers of prose that are known to every student of English Literature are **Jonathan Swift** (1667–1745) and **Laurence Sterne** (1713–68).

Swift was born in Ireland and, although he regarded his return to Dublin as 'banishment', he wrote about the Irish with more fellow feeling, both positive and negative, than did his English contemporaries. In 1720, he argued that Ireland needed economic independence if it was to prosper. In 1729, he produced one of the most witheringly satirical documents in the English language, *A Modest Proposal for Preventing the Children of Poor People from being a Burthen to their Parents or Country*. The tone of the tract is initially calm, urbane and reflective. The writer echoes the viewpoint of the expulsion order against Irish beggars, quoted earlier (Chapter 5), and expresses his sadness at seeing:

> *... the roads and cabin-doors crowded with beggars of the female sex, followed by three, four or six children, all in rags, and importuning ... for an alms.*

Such children have little hope of a decent life. All that they can do is:

> *... turn thieves for want of work, or leave their dear native country, to fight for the Pretender in Spain, or sell themselves to the Barbadoes.*

The solution to the problem is to sell the children, who would provide delicious food:

> *whether stewed, roasted, baked or boiled.*

Such a solution would cut down the population of Irish beggars, provide delicacies for jaded English palates and provide the 'dams' with a small wage.

Swift's *reductio ad absurdum* was meant to make his English readers aware of the conditions to which the native Irish population had been reduced. Critics argue about whether it could have been written by anyone other than Swift, or whether indeed it is the outpouring of a man who was already beginning to show signs of madness. What is certain is that there is nothing else quite like it in literature in English.

Laurence Sterne is mainly remembered for the *Life and Opinions of Tristram Shandy* (1760–61). This work has a verbal extravagance and a stream-of-consciousness mode not matched in English outside the writings of James Joyce or Flann O'Brien. Is this love of linguistic innovation a mark of his Irishness? I would suggest that it is. However, I would have to acknowledge that *Tristram Shandy*, like *A Modest Proposal*, is unique in the English language. Therefore it is not easy to generalise about such a work.

Bless us! – what noble work we should make! – how should I tickle it off? – and what spirits should I find myself in, to be writing away for such readers! – and you, just heaven! – with what raptures would you sit and read, –but oh! – 'tis too much, – I am sick, – I faint away deliciously at the thought of it! – 'tis more than nature can bear! – lay hold of me, – I am giddy, – I am stone blind, –

(Laurence Sterne, *The Life and Opinions of Tristram Shandy, Gentleman*, 229)

Wherein, O wretched company, were ye all deceived for that was the voice of the god that was in a very grievous rage that he would presently lift his arm and spill their souls for their abuses and their spillings done by them contrariwise to his word which forth to bring brenningly biddeth.

(James Joyce, *Ulysses*, 393)

Conclusion of the book, ultimate: Evil is even, truth is an odd number and death is a full stop. When a dog barks late at night and then retires again to bed, he punctuates and gives majesty to the serial enigma of the dark, laying it more evenly and heavily upon the fabric of the mind.

(Flann O'Brien, *At Swim-Two-Birds*, 314)

The nineteenth century produced many Anglo-Irish writers of note but two are worth special mention: **Maria Edgeworth** (1767–1849) and **Lady Sydney Morgan**, who kept her date of birth a secret, although her dates are probably 1785–1859. These two women centred much of their writing on Ireland and are unlike English novelists (and more like American and Australian writers) in preferring the large canvas of several generations to the miniaturist tradition of Jane Austen. Edgeworth is one of the first novelists to recreate accurate dialect speech and she does this mostly without modifying the spelling:

> *'Well, since your honor's honor's so bent upon it, (says I, not willing to cross him, and he in trouble) we must see what we can do.'*

Sir Walter Scott was a fervent admirer of Maria Edgeworth's writing and, in particular, of her ability to recreate the speech patterns of Ireland. He acknowledged his debt to her in the General Preface to the *Waverley* Novels (1829), and commented that 'the extended and well-merited fame of Miss Edgeworth, whose Irish characters have gone so far to make the English familiar with the character of their gay and kind-hearted neighbours in Ireland'. After commenting on her 'rich humour, pathetic tenderness, and admirable tact', he added that he 'felt that something might be attempted for my own country, of the same kind with that which Miss Edgeworth so fortunately achieved for Ireland'.

Edgeworth's Irish novels tend to depict the Anglo-Irish of the 'Big House', a subject tackled with even more insight by **Somerville and Ross** in such novels as *The Real Charlotte* (1894) and *The Big House of Inver* (1925). Lady Morgan, on the other hand, prefers the romantic, idealised Celtic twilight with harps and storms and emotionally-charged atmospheres. Lady Morgan's novels, such as *The Wild Irish Girl* (1806), are not altogether to the modern taste. The characters are idealised and romanticised but they certainly broke the stereotypical mould, where the Irish were described as unintelligent or quick-tempered, or both. Lady Morgan helped her English readers to realise that the Irish had a noble past, a past with a culture and a literature that was unique and inspiring.

> **For those critics who dislike Lady Morgan, preferring the precision and the finesse of Jane Austen, there is an interesting footnote. Many readers of *Mansfield Park* have liked Mary Crawford and have argued that Jane Austen's sudden condemnation of Mary and her brother is structurally unwarranted. Mary Crawford, the attractive, harp-playing Irish woman, is thought to be based on Lady Morgan, a fellow writer who had a much wider readership than her now better-known contemporary.**

The Anglo-Irish poets of the nineteenth and twentieth centuries – and there were many of them – tend to pale into insignificance when measured against the colossus, **W.B. Yeats** (1865–1939). In his early works, he revitalised the myths and legends of ancient warriors like Finn MacCool and Cuchulain, and tragic lovers like Deirdre and Naoise; in his maturity, he wrote of the struggles that our modern world faces; and in between he gave Ireland and the world one of the most memorable pictures of an uprising against a colonial government, in his poem, 'Easter 1916'.

> *Too long a sacrifice*
> *Can make a stone of the heart.*
> *O when may it suffice?*
> *That is Heaven's part, our part*
> *To murmur name upon name,*
> *As a mother names her child*
> *When sleep at last has come*
> *On limbs that had run wild.*
> *What is it but nightfall?*
> *No, no, not night but death;*
> *Was it needless death after all?*
> *For England may keep faith*
> *For all that is done and said.*
>
> *We know their dreams; enough*
> *To know they dreamed and are dead;*
> *And what if excess of love*
> *Bewildered them till they died?*
> *I write it out in a verse –*
> *MacDonagh and MacBride*
> *And Connolly and Pearse*
> *Now and in time to be,*
> *Wherever green is worn,*
> *Are changed, changed utterly:*
> *A terrible beauty is born.*
>
> (W.B Yeats, from 'Easter 1916')

Although Yeats overshadows his contemporaries, **Samuel Ferguson** (1810–86) of Ulster deserves a brief mention. Whereas Yeats introduced an English-speaking world to Irish themes, Ferguson reintroduced the Irish to the 'word cataracts' of medieval Irish poetry. He did this by recreating in English the intricately-woven Irish verse with its assonance, alliteration, rhymes and word compounds, as in such a poem as 'Congal':

> *The deep-clear-watered, foamy crested, terribly-resounding,*
> *Lofty leaping, prone descending, ocean-calf-abounding,*
> *Fishy fruitful, salmon-teeming, many coloured, sunny beaming,*
> *Heady-eddied, horrid thund'ring, ocean-progeny-engend'ring,*
> *Billow-raging, battle-waging, merman-haunted, poet-vaunted,*
> *Royal, patrimonial, old torrent of Eas-Roe.*

If one does not like the complex and the baroque, one may compare Ferguson, unkindly, with the 1970s advertisement for Pepsi:

> *Lipsmackinthirstquenchinacetastinmotivatingoodbuzzincooltalkinhigh*
> *walkin fastlivinnevergivincoolfizzin –PEPSI*

However, one could also link him with Celtic-influenced poets such as **Gerard Manley Hopkins** (1844–89) who, like Swift before him, may have hated the time he spent in Dublin but certainly wrote some of his best poetry there.

A windpuff-bonnet of fawn-froth
Turns and twindles over the broth
Of a pool so pitchblack, fell-frowning,
It rounds and rounds Despair to drowning.

(G.M. Hopkins, 'Inversnaid')

Ferguson was attempting to do the impossible and create, in a variety of modern English, the effervescent love of words that characterised a poetry of a different age and a different language group. Medieval

Irish poets, like the Welsh bards, spoke their poetry aloud. They delighted in creating edifices of sound:

> *The chime and clash of rhyme, alliteration, and assonance, the interplay of vowel and consonant, have been pursued with unfailing zest, sometimes to the detriment of sense and structural quality.*
>
> (Sir Harold Idris Bell, *The Development of Welsh Poetry*, 1936: 5-6)

Nor is such intoxication with word music totally extinct. Francis Hardy, in Brian Friel's *Faith Healer*, knows the power of blending the gnomic and the mnemonic:

> *I'd recite the names to myself just for the mesmerism, the sedation of the incantation.*

It would probably be true to say that the Anglo-Irish writers were supreme among writers in Ireland until the middle of the nineteenth century. By that time, Hiberno-English speakers had sufficient social position and control of a variety of English to express (in a language that was not originally theirs) the longheld thoughts and aspirations that, like the rose, had been forced:

> *... to blush unseen*
> *And waste its sweetness on the desert air.*

Ulster Scots writers

The Ulster Scots also produced their writers, however, most of them virtually unknown outside Northern Ireland. The novelist **W.G. Lyttle** wrote *Betsy Gray: or Hearts of Down* in 1888. The novel uses an idiom that might be thought to be Scots:

> *'What's the matter, Geordie? Why there's no word oot o' yer heid the nicht ava.'*

but the subject matter, the rebellion of 1798 when Catholic and Protestant fought side by side for a free and united Ireland, is quintessentially Irish.

Ulster Scots writers have also written plays, many of them in dialect for dialect speakers. Rarely have the Ulster Scots writers tried to dilute the language, which they feel they share with Robbie Burns. It is, however, the Ulster Scots poetry that touches the most profound chord with many Northern Irish readers. This poetry is often ballad-like and spare. It can deal with the transitoriness of life and love in a poem like 'Coortin'':

> *Time rins awa', an lees us a',*
> *I say, young men, make haste,*
> *Or if you don't, she'll say "she won't"*
> *Whut joys ye'll nivr taste.*

> (Adam Lynn, *Random Rhymes frae Cullybacky*, 1911)

through the strength of feeling of 'The Wee Lassie's First Luve':

> *A cannae hear his name an' hide*
> *My thought wi' ony art:*
> *A cannae see him come, an' calm*
> *The flitterin' uv my heart;*
> *It's pain tae meet him whun A walk,*
> *Or meet him nae ava;*
> *A wish him aye tae come tae me.*
> *A wish him aye awa'*

> (G.F. Savage-Armstrong, *Ballads of Down*, 1901)

to the metaphysical conceits of the hungry beggar, called Holy Bridget, who only longed to feel full:

> *Auld John o' Ralloo wuz sae brid i' the belt,*
> *An sae plump wi' guid leevin' he grew,*
> *That "Holy" wud sigh, "Och, A wush A jist dwelt*
> *In the belly o' John o' Ralloo!"*

> (G.F. Savage-Armstrong)

Ulster Scots poetry is not comfortable poetry. It is rooted in the daily lives of the people who write it and the people who learn it and recite it – often with their own modifications. It does not tend to be written by an elite for an educated readership and, because of its roots in a small community in the north of the island, it remains relatively unknown to outsiders.

Hiberno-English writers

The third group of writers comprehends all those whose ancestral mother tongue was Gaelic. Many of the earliest of these writers were Gaelic speakers first and English users second. Much of their writing may seem more interesting to the historian and the linguist than to the student of literature. Sometimes, as in the ballad *The Boys of Mullaghbawn*, the intricate sound patterns remind us of the claim made about Welsh bards by Idris Bell:

> *Squire Jackson is unequalled*
> *For honour or for reason.*
> *He is not a traitor*
> *To betray the rights of man.*
> *But now we are in danger*
> *From a foul deceitful stranger*
> *That will send for transportation*
> *All the boys of Mullaghbawn.*

The interlinked sounds are only fully apparent when we sing the stanza in the dialect. The underlined syllables all rhyme with 'say'; the 'r' in *Squire* is picked up in *honour, for, betray, rights, are, stranger* and *transportation*; the 's' sound is repeated in *Squire, Jackson, rights, deceitful, stranger, send* and *transportation*; and there are smaller groups as in the 'b' of *betray, but, boys* and *Mullaghbawn* and the 'f' of *for, foul,* and *deceitful*. The more one studies this apparently simple ballad, the more one realises that it may appear 'artless' but the patterns of linked alliteration and assonance to highlight the significant words remind us of the interwoven designs on Irish manuscripts and artefacts.

We could argue about whether **Thomas Moore** (1779–1852) was Anglo-Irish or Hiberno-English in his poetry, and we might well come down on the side of the Anglo-Irish. What we can say, however, is that many of his most beautiful melodies were Irish in origin. In addition, in his best songs, he was able to marry the words and the music to create a perfect entity. This feat is not as easy as is sometimes supposed, as a quotation from the writer **William Carleton** (1794–1869) makes clear. In his *Autobiography*, Carleton describes how his parents were equally at home in Irish and English and that sometimes his mother was asked to sing English words to traditional music:

> *My mother ... had a prejudice against singing the Irish airs to English words ... I remember on one occasion that she was asked to sing the English version of that touching melody "The Red-haired Man's Wife". She replied, "I will sing it for you, but the English words and the air are like a man and his wife quarrelling – the Irish melts into the tune but the English doesn't."*

Until the middle of the nineteenth century, the native Irish were mostly Gaelic-speaking and often their writings in English remind a reader that English was not a first language with them. Even when, by the beginning of the twentieth century, English was a first language, there was a feeling that English 'couldn't quite express us'. This feeling of foreignness is most eloquently summarised by **James Joyce** (1882–1941) when Stephen Daedalus thinks about his use of English and that of 'a countryman of Ben Jonson':

> *The language in which we are speaking is his* before *it is mine. How different are the words* home, Christ, ale, master, *on his lips and mine! I cannot speak or write these words without unrest of spirit. His language, so familiar and so foreign, will always be for me an acquired speech. I have not made or accepted its words. My voice holds them at bay. My soul frets in the shadow of his language.*
>
> (*A Portrait of the Artist as a Young Man*, 1960 ed)

This 'fretting in the shadows' was also, of course, a strength, because Stephen, like Hiberno-English writers, cherished words and played with them in ways not altogether English:

> *Words. Was it their colours? He allowed them to glow and fade, hue after hue ...*
>
> right(A Portrait of the Artist as a Young Man)

Yet, even as James Joyce was creating a character who fretted in the shadow of an Englishman's English, he was shaping a novel that was, and is, unique in the English language. *Ulysses* was originally intended to be a short story but, like Topsy, it 'just growed' and was published in 1922. It is probably the most widely studied book in the language. Even people who have never read it know that it recreates eighteen hours in the lives of three Dublin characters: Leopold Bloom, Molly Bloom, and Stephen Daedalus. Joyce takes the language and stretches it until it becomes capable of caricature, parody, satire, wisdom, dialectal felicity and an apt reflection of the mental processes of very different people. Joyce treats words as if they were notes, capable of both discords and harmonies. And he creates a work that is measurable only against itself. It is, however, an Irish work. The characters could not exist or coexist outside Dublin and the author adds many elements from other languages – including both Irish and Hiberno-English – to create his medium.

A story is told by Frank Budgen in *James Joyce and the Making of Ulyssess* that may be apocryphal but it sheds light on Joyce's search for the perfect place for the precise word. A chance meeting with Joyce is supposed to have gone as follows:

> *I enquired about* Ulysses. *Was it progressing?*
> *'I have been working hard on it all day,' said Joyce.*
> *'Does that mean that you have written a great deal?' I said.*
> *'Two sentences,' said Joyce.*
> *I looked sideways but Joyce was not smiling. I thought of Flaubert.*
> *'You have been seeking the* mot juste*?' I said.*
> *'No,' said Joyce. 'I have the words already. What I am seeking is the*

perfect order of words in the sentence. There is an order in every way appropriate. I think I have it.

(F. Budgen, *James Joyce and the Making of Ulysses*, 1934:20)

After Joyce, all Hiberno-English writers suffered one setback: it was hard not to write their own version of *A Portrait*. They also, however, experienced such consciousness-raising that never again did young writers feel that they needed to fret in the shadow of anyone's language.

Since the Second World War, Hiberno-English speakers have produced so many highly regarded writers that the rest of this chapter could degenerate into a list. **Seamus Heaney** has been admired, as, perhaps the most mellifluous and gifted of late twentieth-century poets; **Frances Molloy's** *No Mate for the Magpie* is a celebration of the Derry dialect and the strength of character that can rise above bigotry and prejudice, poverty and mental breakdown; and **Brian Friel** in *Translations* has given the world a play that raises issues normally confined to serious debate – issues such as the loss of a language and with it the loss of a way of life, a culture, and a unique vision of the world.

Roddy Doyle comes, in theory, from the same background as other Dublin Hiberno-English writers and yet he is different. If there is a novel equal to his comic *Paddy Clarke Ha Ha Ha*, it is probably Irvine Welsh's Glaswegian novel, *Trainspotters*, rather than anything written in Ireland. Doyle was born into an independent country where the English language was the norm, and brought up in a society where television was probably a greater influence on people's lives than the Irish language. Of course, Roddy Doyle sounds Irish when he speaks and he uses Hiberno-English words and structures. However, he is also a product of an English-using world, someone who happened to be born in Dublin rather than in Glasgow or New York or Melbourne. Increasingly, young Irish writers are exploring international themes. It may be 'The Death by heroin of Sid Vicious' for **Paul Durcan** or 'The Indians on Alcatraz' for **Paul Muldoon**. It is not that such writers are turning their back on Ireland or on a Gaelic world view. Rather, they are members of a world literature club, to which the English language is the key.

The existence of writers such as Roddy Doyle, whose medium is unashamedly English, reminds us that radio, films and television have helped to produce a generation of people in Ireland who are much less insular in their outlook than their parents were. If we take a global perspective, this is undoubtedly a positive step. However, it is a step that may lead as inexorably to the death of Irish Gaelic as to the death of hundreds of other minority languages world-wide. This point is true of the languages of Cameroon in West Africa or of Fiji in the South Pacific just as it is of Irish Gaelic in Ireland or Breton in France. Although it is outside the brief of this book, we might seriously consider the possibility that English has two faces: the benign aspect that permits communication and understanding between different peoples in every country on the planet; and the obverse where the English language is as deadly as a virus, destroying cultures that 'English could not comprehend'. Most speakers and writers in Ireland have, largely unconsciously, chosen English as their medium. It is perhaps left to the philosophers to ponder about the losses and gains of giving up a language 'opulent with tomorrows' in favour of the most useful trade language the world has ever known.

On a tributary of the Amazon
an Indian boy
steps out of the forest
and strikes up on a flute.

Imagine my delight
when we cut the outboard motor
and I recognize the strains
of 'The Lass of Aughrim'

'He hopes,' Jesus explains,
'to charm
fish from the water

on what was the tibia
of a priest
from a long-abandoned Mission.'

(Paul Muldoon, 'The Lass of Aughrim', 1987)

Looking Back in Sorrow

... the world has become much smaller and we should now view ourselves not in an insular but in a world context ... The canvas can be as small as you wish, but the more accurately you write and the more truthful you are the more validity your play will have for the world.

(Des Hickey and Gus Smith, *A Paler Shade of Green*, 1972: 233)

Green English has looked briefly at the Englishes that Ireland has learned and modified and helped to spread around the world. Forms of English have been spoken and written on the island for over eight hundred years, making Irish English one of the oldest varieties in the world. Our voyage of exploration has allowed us to glimpse the contacts of the past, to see more clearly the legacy of the seventeenth-century English and the Scots, and to focus on the grafted English that allowed the Irish to communicate with their colonisers and yet still keep alive their Gaelic world view. The spectrum of Englishes in Ireland was forged into Green English, a unique amalgam that is, in the words of the Nigerian, Chinua Achebe:

... sufficiently different from English to allow us to express our own cultural dreams and aspirations, but sufficiently similar to allow communication among all the English speakers in the world.

Having English, of whatever density of Green, has allowed Irish speakers to continue to feel Irish and yet to communicate easily and productively with the one in five human beings on our planet who regularly use English for some of their communication needs.

The three varieties of English in Ireland, Anglo-Irish, Ulster Scots and Hiberno-English, taken together, form 'Green English'. Recent recorded conversations and narratives, especially of people under forty, suggest that Irish English is increasingly moving towards international norms. In this, it reflects the third wave of English influence: the influence of living in an English-using world. As children are educated in state schools with essentially the same syllabus, the same examinations and the same exposure to the media, their English is being internationalised. The Irish Gaelic substratum that survived in Hiberno-English is beginning to disappear. People throughout the island are increasingly speaking with a modified local accent; they are learning the standard vocabulary and, gradually, they are absorbing standard structures and expressions. They are, in addition, discarding Gaelic-influenced pronunciations, words, rhythms and idioms.

If this trend continues, then in one or two generations, most of the native Gaelic elements found in Hiberno-English will have disappeared. And perhaps such a scenario should be welcomed. If people are not differentiated by their linguistic preferences, is it possible that centuries of division and discord can be healed?

Perhaps.

But there is a price to pay, whatever route we follow. In his play *Translations*, Brian Friel dramatises the loss of a mother tongue. Through his characters, he suggests that English people and Irish people are as different as their languages. English, he suggests is ideally suited to commerce (p. 25) but 'couldn't really express us'. Irish Gaelic is, on the other hand:

> *A rich language ... You'll find that some cultures expend on their vocabularies and syntax acquisitive energies and ostentations entirely lacking in their material lives ... a rich language ... full of the mythologies of fantasy and hope and self-deception – a syntax opulent with tomorrows. It is our response to mud cabins and a diet of potatoes. (p. 42)*

'Commerce' may not sound as culturally rich as 'mythologies', but commerce is wealth-creating, whereas a language that deals in 'tomorrows' may be unsatisfactory in coping with 'today'.

In Ireland in the past, the indigenous people clung to their religion, their culture and their traditions, and they were able to do so because the English they adopted was essentially a 'grafted' English. Its structures and idiom were sufficiently close to their ancestral mother tongue to allow them to respond to life in very much the same way that their ancestors had done. They may have failed to absorb the post-sixteenth century English and Scottish settlers, but neither had the settlers managed to absorb them. Until now.

Many Hiberno-English speakers worry that the younger generations are losing their Irishness, losing contact with the stem onto which the English language was grafted, and are becoming virtually indistinguishable from English speakers in England or Australia or the United States. Few of these people have read Sapir or Whorf, but many of them worry that, in losing their linguistic roots, they are losing their Irish way of thinking, losing a world view that sustained them in the past. Of course, Irish Gaelic is officially sanctioned in the Republic of Ireland and is taught in all schools, but few people, even in government circles, would claim that the country's language policies have produced a bilingual population. The strength of feeling towards a Gaelic culture is, in part, expressed in the desire to give Irish names to children. It is also expressed in the serious attempts being made to reinvigorate Gaelic in the Republic of Ireland and to reintroduce it as a mother tongue in the North. The renewed desire to keep Gaelic alive is a partial response to a feeling that, if the Hiberno-English halfway house is no longer an option, then children should be encouraged to be active bilinguals. If bilingualism could become a reality, not a dream, then the language and the culture will perhaps not ebb away to become only a shadow in the minds of the old.

Will the Republic's educational policy and Northern Ireland's dreams of reviving Gaelic succeed? Will Irish people be able to revive a dying language and a disappearing culture? Only time will tell. It is, of course, not even certain that the problems many Irish people see are, in any way, related to language. In the last fifty years, virtually all speakers of Green English have become more affluent, more educated, more widely travelled. They have also become less religious, less interested in the extended family, less willing to accept the status quo. Such changes may have little or nothing to do with language. And, perhaps, the people who lament the passing of Irish Gaelic and its close relative Hiberno-English are really lamenting the modern condition. What remains true, however, is that many Irish people have a paradoxical attitude to the English they use. They love its usefulness, its versatility, its flexibility, and they feel a little ashamed of the speed with which they abandoned their Gaelic tongue. For better or worse, however, they have adopted the Other Tongue. And they are using it with a vigour and power that has resulted in the production of some of the finest literature in the English language.

> Many people in Northern Ireland dream of reintroducing Irish Gaelic as a living, every-day language. Evening and weekend Gaelic classes are held in both Belfast and Derry and some communities have gone further. Coalisland, a small town in Tyrone, has established a *Bunscoil*, where children receive nursery education through the medium of Irish.

Yet skill and versatility in English does not, and should not, preclude the survival of Irish Gaelic. Somehow we must learn to provide Gaelic in a format that is attractive to people entering the third millennium. And if we don't, we may have a price to pay. Writing about translation, George Steiner makes the strong claim:

> *The point is always the same: ash is no translation of fire.*
> (*After Babel*, 1976: 241)

If we lose both Irish Gaelic and Hiberno-English, we may indeed learn the truth of such words.

The Irish language should be saved, and indeed must be saved, but this does not mean discarding or discrediting English, because English, in its green form, has entered deep into the psyche of the Irish people. One of the clearest indications of just how deep can be gauged by calling to mind the last hours Patrick Pearse (1879–1916), a poet, a patriot, and a gentle man, who genuinely

seems to have believed that Ireland could turn the clock back, reintroduce Irish Gaelic and make the country, once again, an island of
saints and scholars. On the night before he was executed after the
Easter Rising of 1916, he wrote a poem called 'The Wayfarer' – and
the poem was entirely in English:

The beauty of the world hath made me sad,
This beauty that will pass;
Sometimes my heart hath shaken with great joy
To see a leaping squirrel in a tree,
Or a red ladybird upon a stalk,
Or little rabbits in a field at evening,
Lit by a slanting sun,
Or some green hill where shadows drifted by,
Some quiet hill where mountainy men hath sown
And soon would reap; near to the gate of heaven;
Of children with bare feet upon the sands
Of some ebbed sea, or playing on the streets
Of little towns in Connacht,
Things young and happy,
And then my heart hath told me:
These will pass,
Will pass and change, will die and be no more,
Things bright and green, things young and happy;
And I have gone upon my way
Sorrowful.

Bibliography

Astley, T., ed. (1760): *Collection of Voyages and Travels*, London, J. Coote.

Atiya, A.S. (1968): *A History of Eastern Christianity*, London, Methuen.

Avis, W.S. (1965): *A Bibliography of Writings on Canadian English (1857–1965)*, Toronto, Gage.

Ayling, R. ed. (1985): *Seven Plays by Seán O'Casey*, London, Macmillan.

Badawy, A. (1978): *Coptic Art and Archaeology*, Cambridge, Massachusetts, MIT Press.

Bailey, R.W. and M. Görlach, eds. (1982): *English as a World Language*, Ann Arbor, University of Michigan Press.

Baker, S. (1966): *The Australian Language*, Sydney, Currawong.

Barber, C. (1993): *The English Language: A Historical Introduction*, Cambridge, Cambridge University Press.

Barbot, J. (1746): 'A Description of the coasts of North and South Guinea', in *A Collection of Voyages and Travels*, Vol. 5, eds. J. and A. Churchill, London, Henry Linton and John Osborn.

Bauer, L. (1994): *Watching English Change*, London, Longman.

Baugh, A.C. (1959): *A History of the English Language*, 2nd ed., London, Routledge and Kegan Paul.

Beckett, J.C. (1966): *The Making of Modern Ireland 1600–1923*, London, Faber and Faber.

Beckett, J.C. (1979): *A Short History of Ireland*, London, Hutchinson.

Bell, H.I. (1936): *The Development of Welsh Poetry*, Oxford, Clarendon Press.

Bliss, A.J. (1979): *Spoken English in Ireland 1600–1740*, Dublin, Dolmen Press.

Boatner, M.T. and J.E. Gates (1976): *A Dictionary of American Idioms*, (revised by Adam Makkai), Woodbury, Barron's Books.

Braidwood, J. (1964): 'Ulster and Elizabethan English', *Ulster Dialects*, ed. G.B. Adams, Holywood, Ulster Folk Museum.

Brophy, B., ed. (1986): *Lady Morgan's The Wild Irish Girl*, London, Pandora.

Budgen, F. (1934): *James Joyce and the Making of Ulysses*, London, Grayson and Grayson.

Burchfield, R., ed. (1986): *The Oxford English Dictionary*, rev. Oxford, Oxford University Press.

Butler, S. (1932 ed.): *Erewhon*, London, Dent.

Carleton, W. (1968 ed.): *Autobiography*, London, MacGibbon and Kee.

Carlyle, T. (1897 ed.): *Oliver Cromwell's Letters and Speeches*, London, Chapman and Hall.

Carney, J. (1985): *Medieval Irish Lyrics* with *The Irish Bardic Poet*, Dublin, Dolmen Press.

Carroll, J.B. (1956): *Language, Thought and Reality: Selected Writings of Benjamin Lee Whorf*, New York, Technology Press of MIT.

Cassidy, F.G., ed. (1985–): *Dictionary of American Regional English*, vols 1–3. Cambridge, Mass., Belknap Press.

Chambers, J.K., ed. (1975): *Canadian English: Origins and Structures*, London, Methuen.

Committee on Irish Language Attitudes Research (1975): *Report*, Dublin, CILAR.

Clarke, W.S. (1955): *The Early Irish Stage: The Beginnings to 1720*, London, Oxford University Press.

Craig, M. (1969): *Dublin 1660-1860*, Dublin, Allen Figgis.

Craigie, W. (1931–72): *A Dictionary of the Older Scottish Tongue*, Milford, Oxford University Press.

Curtis, L.P. (1971): *Apes and Angels: The Irishman in Victorian Caricature*, Newton Abbot, David and Charles.

Crystal, D. (1988): *The English Language*, London, Penguin.

Dalrymple, W. (1998): *From the Holy Mountain*, London, Flamingo.

Dampier, W. (1697): *A New Voyage Round the World*, London, James Knapton.

Davenport, C.B. and M. Steggerda (1929): *Race Crossing in Jamaica*, Washington, Carnegie Institution.

De Bhaldraithe, T. (1959): *English-Irish Dictionary*, Dublin, An Gúm, An Roinn Oideachais.

Dineen, P.S. (1927): *Foclóir Gaedhilge agus Béarla*, Dublin, Irish Texts Society.

Dobson, E.J. (1968): *English Pronunciation 1500–1700*, Oxford, Clarendon Press.

Dohan, M.H. (1974): *Our Own Words*, New York, Knopf.

Donnan, E. (1930–35): *Documents Illustrative of the Slave Trade*, Vols 1–4, Washington, Carnegie Institution.

Edgeworth, M. (1800): *Castle Rackrent*, reprinted by the Norton Library, New York, W.W. Norton and Co., 1965.

Edwards, B. (1807): *The History, civil and commercial, of the British Colonies of the West Indies*, London, Stockdale.

Elliott, H. (1988): *Contemporary Women Writers in the North of Ireland*, unpublished dissertation, University of Leeds.

Ellis, S.G. (1985): *Tudor Ireland*, London, Longman.

Farquhar, G. – See Stonehill

Ferguson, C.A. and S.B. Heath, eds. (1981): *Language in the USA*, Cambridge, Cambridge University Press.

Francis, W. N. (1974): *The English Language*, Surrey, The English Universities Press Ltd.

Fraser, M. (1974): *Children in Conflict*, Harmondsworth, Penguin.

Friel, B. (1981): *Translations*, London, Faber and Faber.

Garcia, O. and R. Otheguy (1989): *English across Cultures: Cultures across English*, Berlin, Mouton de Gruyter.

Gardner, W.H. and N.H. MacKenzie (1970): *The Poems of Gerard Manley Hopkins*, London, Oxford University Press.

George, M.D. (1930): *London Life in the Eighteenth Century*, London, K. Paul, Trench, Trubner.

Godley, A.D., ed. (1915): *The Poetical Works of Thomas Moore*, London, Oxford University Press.

Gore, M. (1851): *On the Dwellings of the Poor*, London, Saunders and Otley

Graham, W. (1980): *The Scots Word Book*, Edinburgh, Ramsay Head Press.

Greene, D. (1966): *The Irish Language*, Dublin, Cultural Relations Committee of Ireland.

Hakluyt, R. (1972 ed.): *Voyages and Discoveries*, edited and abridged by Jack Beeching. Harmondsworth, Penguin.

Hancock, I.F. (1987): *Land of Pain*, Ann Arbor, Karoma.

Harlow, V.T. (1926): *History of Barbados 1625–1685*, London, Oxford University Press.

Harris, J., D. Little and D. Singleton (1986): *Perspectives on the English Language in Ireland*, Dublin, Centre for Language and Communication, TCD.

Harris, W. (1747): *Hibernica or some antient pieces relating to Ireland*.

Heaney, M. (1994): *Over Nine Waves*, London, Faber and Faber.

Hewitt J. (1968): *Collected Poems*, London, Macgibbon and Kee.

Hickey, D. and G. Smith, (1972): *A Paler Shade of Green*, London, Frewin.

Hill, G. (1873): *Historical Account of the Plantation of Ulster 1608–1620*, Belfast, McCaw, Stevenson and Orr.

Hogan, J.J. (1927): *The English Language in Ireland*, Dublin, The Educational Company of Ireland.

Holm, J. and A. Shilling (1982): *Dictionary of Bahamian English*, Cold Spring, Lexik House.

Hopkins, G.M. – See Gardner and MacKenzie

Horn, W. (1991): 'On the Origin of the Celtic Cross' in W. Horn, J. White Marshall and G.D. Rourke (eds), *The Forgotten Hermitage of Skelling Michael*, Berkeley, University of California Press.

Hughes, A. (1949): *Early Mediaeval Music up to 1300*, Oxford, Oxford University Press.

Hume, A. (1864): *Essays on Down and Antrim*, Belfast, Newsletter Office.

Hume, A. (1878): *Remarks on the Irish Dialect of the English Language*, Liverpool, Collegiate Institute.

Hutchinson, W.R. (1951): *Tyrone Precinct*, Belfast, W. Erskine Mayne.

Hyde, D. (1967 ed.): *A Literary History of Ireland: From Earliest Times to the Present Day*, London, Ernest Benn Ltd.,

Jeffares, A.N. (1982): *Anglo-Irish Literature*, London, Macmillan.

Jeffares, A.N. (1984): *Poems of W.B. Yeats: A New Selection*, London, Macmillan.

Jeffares, A.N. (1986): *Parameters of Irish Literature in English*, Gerrards Cross, Colin Smythe.

Joyce, J. (1960): *A Portrait of the Artist as a Young Man*, Harmondsworth, Penguin.

Joyce, J. (1969): *Ulysses*, Harmondsworth, Penguin.

Joyce, P.W. (1910): *English as We Speak It in Ireland*, London, Longmans, Green, and Co.

Kavanagh, P.J. (1987): *Presences*, London, Chatto and Windus.

Kinsella, T., ed. (1986): *The New Oxford Book of Irish Verse*, Oxford, Oxford University Press.

Keating, G. (1902–14): *A General History of Ireland*, London, The Irish Texts Society.

Kee, R. (1980): *A History of Ireland*, London, Weidenfeld and Nicholson.

Lentzner, C. (1891): *Colonial English: a glossary of Australian, Anglo-Indian, Pidgin English, West Indian and South African Words*, London, Kegan Paul.

Le Page, R.B. and D. De Camp (1960): *Jamaican Creole*, London, Methuen.

Lewis, T. (n.d.): *These Seventy Years*, London, Carey Press.

Ludowyk, F. (1998): 'Ab(h)ominable (H)aitch', *Ozwords*, Canberra, Australian National University.

Lynn, A. (1911): *Random Rhymes frae Cullybacky*, Belfast, W. & G. Baird.

Lyttle, W.G. (1888): *Betsy Gray or Hearts of Down: A Tale of Ninety-Eight*, Bangor, Co. Down, W.G. Lyttle.

McArthur, T. (1998): *The English Languages*, Cambridge, Cambridge University Press.

McCrum, R., W. Cran and R. MacNeil (1986): *The Story of English*, London, Faber and Faber.

McIlroy, R. (n.d.): *A Concise History of the Stuart Period*, Dublin and Belfast, The Educational Company of Ireland Ltd.

MacLeod, I. and P. Cairns (1993): *The Concise English-Scots Dictionary*, Edinburgh, W.& R. Chambers.

McNamara, J., ed. (1967): *Problems of Bilingualism*, special issue of *Journal of Social Issues* 23: 2.

Magee, J. (1974): *Northern Ireland: Crisis and Conflict*, London, Routledge & Kegan Paul.

Magnusson, M. and H. Pålsson (1965): *The Vinland Sagas*, Harmondsworth, Penguin.

Makins, M., ed. (1995): *The Collins Gem Scots Dictionary*, London, HarperCollins.

Malone, A.E. (1929): *The Irish Drama 1896–1928*, London, Constable.

Maxwell, D.E.S. (1984): *A Critical History of Modern Irish Drama*, Cambridge, Cambridge University Press.

Meyer, K. (1897): *Imram Brain: The Voyage of Bran*, London, David Nutt.

Molloy, F. (1985): *No Mate for the Magpie*, London, Virago Press.

Montague, J., ed. (1974): *The Faber Book of Irish Verse*, London, Faber and Faber.

Moody, T.W. (1974): *The Ulster Question 1603–1973*, Dublin, Mercier Press.

Moore – see Godley.

Muldoon, P. (1987): *Meeting the British*, London, Faber and Faber.

Murphy, G. (1956): *Early Irish Lyrics*, Oxford, Clarendon Press.

New, M. and J. New, eds. (1978): *The Life and Opinions of Tristram Shandy Gentleman*, Florida, University Press of Florida.

Noble, C.F. (1747): *Voyage to the East Indies in 1747 and 1748*, London.

O'Brien, F. (1976): *At Swim-Two-Birds*, London, Hart-Davis MacGibbon.

O'Casey, S. – See Ayling.

O Cúiv, B. (1961): *Seven Centuries of Irish Learning*, Dublin, Stationery Office.

O Cúiv, B., ed. (1969): *A View of the Irish Language*, Dublin, Stationery Office.

O Muirithe, D., ed. (1977): *The English Language in Ireland*, Dublin and Cork, Mercier Press.

Oskamp, H.P.A. (1970): *The Voyage of Mael Duin*, Groningen, Wolters-Noordhoff.

Oxford English Dictionary, London, Oxford University Press, 1933, and *Oxford English Dictionary Supplement*, 1986.

Patterson, D. (1860): *The Provincialisms of Belfast*, Belfast, Mayne.

Paulin, T. (1983): *A New Look at the Language Question*, Derry, Field Day Theatre Company Limited.

Price, A.G. (1939): *White Settlers in the Tropics*, New York, American Geographical Society.

Purchas, S. (1625): *Purchas his Pilgrimes*, London, William Stansby for Henrie Fetherstone.

Quinn, D.B. (1973): *Ralegh and the British Empire*, London, Pelican.

Savage-Armstrong, G.F. (1901): *Ballads of Down*, London, Longmans, Green and Co.

Skeat, W.W. (1911): *English Dialects from the Eighth Century to the Present Day*, Cambridge, Cambridge University Press.

Smith, G. and D. Hickey (1972): *A Paler Shade of Green*, London, Frewin.

Spenser, E. (1596, 1934 ed.): *A View of the State of Ireland*, London, Eric Partridge.

Steiner, G. (1975): *After Babel: Aspects of Language and Translation*, London, Oxford University Press.

Stenson, N. (1981): *Studies in Irish Syntax*, Tubingen, Gunter Narr Verlag.

Stonehill, C. ed. (1930): *The Complete Works of George Farquhar*, London, Nonesuch.

Story, G., W. Kirwin, and J. Widdowson (1982): *Dictionary of Newfoundland English*, Toronto, University Press.

Strang, B. (1974): *A History of English*, London, Methuen.

Swift, R. and S. Gilley, eds. (1986): *The Irish in the Victorian City*, London, Croom Helm.

Synge, J.M. (1968 ed.): *Collected Works*, London, Oxford University Press.

Thurneysen, R. (1949): *A Grammar of Old Irish*, Dublin, The Dublin Institute for Advanced Studies.

Todd, L. (1984): 'By their words divided', *English World-Wide*, *5.2*, Amsterdam, Benjamins.

Todd, L. (1989): *The Language of Irish Literature*, London, Macmillan.

Todd, L. (1990): *Words Apart: A Dictionary of Northern Ireland English*, Gerrards Cross, Colin Smythe.

Todd, L. (1997): *Dictionary of English Usage*, London, Cassell.

Trudgill, P. and J.Hannah (1982): *International English*, London, Edward Arnold.

Trudgill, P. and J. Hannah (1984): *Language in the British Isles*, Cambridge, Cambridge University Press.

Turner, G. (1966): *The English Language in Australia and New Zealand*, London, Longmans.

Von Hamel, A.G. (1912): 'On Anglo-Irish Syntax', *Englische Studien 45*, Leipzig.

Wakelin, M. (1972): *English Dialects: An Introduction*, London, Athlone Press.

Welch, R. ed. (1996): *Oxford Companion to Irish Literature*, Oxford, Oxford University Press.

Wells, J.C. (1982): *Accents of English*, vols 1-3, Cambridge, Cambridge University Press.

Wilson, J. (1915): *Lowland Scotch*, London, Oxford University Press.

Woodham-Smith, C. (1962): *The Great Hunger*, London, Hamish Hamilton.

Wright, J., ed. (1898): *The English Dialect Dictionary*, London, Henry Frowde.

Wright, P., ed. (1966): *Lady Nugent's Journal of her Residence in Jamaica from 1801–1805*, Kingston, Institute of Jamaica.

Dictionary

The influence of the Celtic languages on English has traditionally been described as 'slight'. One of the themes of this book is that the influence has been underestimated in three main ways:

➤ Authorities like the *Oxford English Dictionary* have preferred to list an item as 'etymology unknown' rather than to search the Celtic languages for word origins. Often, indeed, they claim without any supporting evidence that Celtic words that are similar to English words come from English. We provide two examples of this bias.

The first is the word **bodkin**, 'a short knife':

[Of unknown etymology: the orig. form in Eng. was *boydekin*, *boidekyn*, in 3 syllables. The form naturally suggests a dim. in *-kin*: but no primitive of the required form appears in Eng. or other related language. The phonetic history is also difficult.

(In default of finding it elsewhere, the derivation has been sought in Celtic. The Welsh *bi'dogyn* 'little dagger', fixed on by some, must be discarded, both because it is accented on the penult, and because the ME. word was itself adopted in Welsh as *bwytkin*; but some still think it possible that *boydekin* may have originated in some kind of corruption of Ir. *bideog*, Gael. *biodag*, Welsh *bidog* dagger.)]

The second example is **cog**, 'One of a series of teeth or similar projections on the circumference of a wheel':

[ME. *cogge*, found from 13th c.: the Sw. *kugge*, Norw. *kug*, pl. *kugger*, in same sense, are evidently cognate; but the relations between them are not determined.

The Celtic words, Ir., Gael. *cog*, Welsh *cocas*, uncritically cited as the prob. source, are (as usual in such cases) from English ...]

Creolists have pointed out that people in contact situations often use words that come from two or more of the languages involved. Thus West African Pidgin English uses *doti* for 'dirt, earth', and *uman* or *wuman* for 'woman'. Early students of the language claimed that these words were from English 'dirty' and 'woman'. However, scholars with a knowledge of African languages pointed out that the word for 'earth, soil, dirt' in Twi is *doté* and the word for 'woman' in Efik is *uman*. (Few people would suggest that the Efik people did not have women before the arrival of the English!)

If there are fortuitous resemblances between African and European languages – and there are – then it stands to reason that there must have been even more similarities between the Celtic languages of Britain and the Germanic languages that were carried to England by the Angles, Saxons and Jutes. Yet these resemblances, or multiple etymologies, have never been included in any assessment of the influence of Celtic languages on English.

The Irish have carried English around the world since the sixteenth century. Their use of English is likely to have affected the English spoken by people in the Americas and Australia, in particular. They carried not only Irish words and Irish-influenced words and phrases, but also English words in a form that had largely died out in England but had been preserved in Ireland.

The Dictionary that follows is not meant to be comprehensive. It merely offers a number of items used in Ireland and in other parts of the world. It provides etymologies, indicates whether the word is from Irish Gaelic (G), from English (E) or from English dialects preserved in Ireland (EI). Readers are invited to examine them and assess the validity of the claims. The quotations are either from literature or from recorded dialogue.

A

able adj., 'fit for, able to cope with'
G: *ábalta*, 'able, able to cope with'
E: *able*
I'm not able for the oul' stairs these days.
There was a time I could lep them, but
they have me bate now.

above adv., 'up'
G: *thuas*, 'above'
E: *above*
He's above on the roof, fixing the loose
slates.
the man above = God, an fear thuas

abroad adv., 'outside, away from the
house'
G: *amuigh*, 'outside, abroad'
E: *abroad*
It's abroad she is, looking for the oul' cat.

ach, och inter. + reinforcement of 'but'
G: *ach(t)*, 'but'
E: *ach, och*, interjection
Och! but I'm tired of mist and dark,
And roads where there's never a house nor
bush,
And tired I am of bog and road
And the crying wind and the lonesome hush!
(Padraic Colum, 'The Old Woman of
the Road')

acushla voc., 'darling'
G: *a chuisle*, 'pulse'
Remove him, acushla.
(James Joyce, *Ulysses*)

afear(e)d adj., 'frightened'
EI: *afear* + *-ed*.
Used over 30 times by Shakespeare, but
rare in literature after 1700, having
been supplanted by 'afraid'. Interestingly, Chaucer seems to distinguish
between 'afraid' and 'afeared' as many
Irish people do.

This wyf was not affered ne affrayed.
(Chaucer, *Shipman's Tale*)
Don't be afraid, chile. I'm afeared(d) o'
nobody, nether God, Man nor the Holy
Ghost.

afore adv., 'before'
EI: *a-* (prefix) + *fore*.
Get the place red(d) up [tidied] *afore they*
come.

after aspect marker indicating recent
completion
G: *i ndiaidh, tar éis*, 'after' as in *Tá sé i*
ndiaidh sin a dheanamh, 'He has just
done that' (lit. Be he after that
doing.)
E: *after*
Sure I'm after seeing him not five minutes
ago.
(James Joyce, *Ulysses*)

again adv., 'on another occasion'
G: *arís*, 'again, on a future occasion'
E: *again*
I've no money on me. I'll have to see you
again.

airy adj., 'haunted'
G: *aerach*, 'haunted'
E: etymology unknown
The English word *eerie* was probably
borrowed from Scots Gaelic.
Up the airy mountain
Down the rushy glen,
We daren't go a hunting
For fear of little men.
(William Allingham, 'The Fairies')

al(l)anna voc., 'darling'
G: *a leanbh*, 'child, darling'
An' what is it you're thinkin' of, allanna?
(Seán O'Casey, *Juno and the Paycock*,
Scene ii)
SEE: **child**

ass noun, 'donkey'

G: *asal*, 'donkey'

E: etymology unknown (The *Oxford English Dictionary* points out that 'the Old Northumbrian *asal, assal, assald*' is from a Celtic source and adds that *ass* is perhaps a 'diminutive' of this.)

He knows the place as well as a begging ass.

asshole voc., noun, 'fool', 'someone from the back of beyond'

G: *asal*, 'donkey'

E: *hole*

The man has no sense. He's an asshole.
I'm from the asshole o' nowhere [i.e. the back of beyond, from the remotest of remote areas]

asthore voc., 'darling'

G: *a stóir mo chroí, 'my heart's treasure'*

And there she was right enough, that lovely sight enough, the girleen bawn asthore…

(James Joyce, *Finnegan's Wake*)

SEE: **store**

B

back noun, 'part of the body adjacent to the spinal axis'

G: *bac*, 'support'

E: *back*

God, at our back in times of need.

ballyhoo noun, verb, 'uproar, blatant publicity'

G: *bailiú*, 'gathering of people'

It wasn't so much of a kehoin' as a ballyhoo.

banjaxed verb, 'ruined, destroyed'

G: etymology uncertain, perhaps from *bandaírne*, 'disappointed person'

E: etymology unknown

Here is his black heart sitting there as large as life in the middle of the pulp of his banjaxed corpse.

(Flann O'Brien, At *Swim-two-Birds*)

bannock noun, 'loaf of bread, usually of oatmeal'

G: *bannach*, 'oatmeal loaf'

A wee bannock in your hand an' a drop of milk was your breakfast.

banshee noun, 'fairy woman whose wailing foretells a death'

G: *bean sidhe*, 'fairy woman'

Down the lane-way of the popular banshees

(Patrick Kavanagh, 'Out after Dark')

banter noun and verb, 'humorous ridicule' formerly slang term for 'ridicule'

G: etymology uncertain, perhaps from *bonnduirc*, 'churl, cheat'

E etymology uncertain

Peter's Banter (as he calls it in his Alsatia phrase) upon transubstantiation.

(Jonathan Swift, *Tale of a Tub*)

bar noun, 'the slightest amount', 'the latest gossip'

G: *bearraí*, 'shred, slice'

E: etymology unknown

I haven't heard a bar all day.

barmbrack noun, 'bread with currants in it'

G: *báirín breac*, 'speckled loaf'

Barm-bracks was always baked at Hallow-een and your mother put things inside, like a ring, or a small coin.

Both barmhearts shall become yeastcake by their brackfest.

(James Joyce, *Finnegan's Wake*)

barrack verb, 'brag, noisy criticism'
G: etymology uncertain, perhaps from *barracht*, 'superiority'
E: etymology unknown
To use a football phrase, they all to a man 'barrack' for the British Lion.
(*Melbourne Punch* 14 Aug, 1890)

bat noun and verb, 'wooden stick or club used in games'
G: *bata*, 'stick, cudgel'
E: etymology unknown
We played bat and ball and cat and bat.

bawn noun, 'enclosure'
G: *bábhún*, 'enclosure for cattle'
E: etymology unknown
These ... bawns which you see so strongly trenched and thrown up.
(Edmund Spenser, *A View of the Present State of Ireland*, 1596)

be verb, 'be'
G: *bí*, as in *Bí ciuin* = Be quiet
The structure 'do(es) be' reflects Irish Gaelic usage and has been carried worldwide by the Irish.
E: *be*
I know you're a friend of his, not like some of those others he does be with.
(James Joyce, *Dubliners*)

blarney noun, 'flattery, sweet talk'
Irish placename: Blarney, Co Cork
You do not want to come here every day to listen to a lot of blarney.
(*Times* 18 June, 1955)

blather noun and verb, 'talk nonsense, babble', 'person who talks nonsense'
G: *bladair*, 'flattery, coax'
E: from Norse *blaðra*, 'nonsense'
Will you stop your blatherin' for a minute, man.
(Seán O'Casey, *The Plough and the Stars*)

bludgeon noun and verb, 'short stick or club', 'beat someone severely'
G: uncertain etymology, perhaps related to *blaodhach*, 'crying out, shouting'
E: etymology unknown
The battle of the 28th was fair bludgeon work.
(Duke of Wellington, Letter, 5 August, 1813)

bodhrán, bowraun noun, 'tambourine-like drum'
G: *bodhrán*, 'drum'
the wail of tin
whistle ... and
the bodhrán begins
(John Montague, 'The Lure')

bodkin, noun, 'short knife, dagger'
G: *bideóg* + *ín*, 'dagger + diminutive'
E: etymology unknown
For who would bear the whips and scorns of time ...
When he might his quietus make
With a bare bodkin?
(Shakespeare, *Hamlet*)

body noun, 'person'
G: *bodach*, 'clown'
E: etymology uncertain
What do you din a body's ears for?
(R.B. Sheridan, *Trip to Scarborough*, 1777)

bog noun, 'soft, marshy ground'
G: *bogach*, 'bog', *bog*, 'soft'
... an' not boyos that's only afther comin' up from the bog of Allen.
(Seán O'Casey, *Juno and the Paycock*)

bold adj., 'naughty'
G: *dána*, 'bold, forward, shameless'
E: *bold*, 'brave'

You'll get what Paddy gave the drum [i.e.
a good beating] *if you don't stop being so
bold.*

bonnyclabber, bonnyclobber noun,
'thick milk, curds'
G: *bainne clabair*, 'thick milk'
No dollop this, but thick rich bonnyclabber.
(James Joyce, *Ulysses*)

boxty noun, 'reheated leftover food,
mess'
G: *bacstaí*, 'bread made from leftover
potatoes'
What's that boxty you're playing with?

boycott, noun and verb 'refuse to co-
operate'
E: surname, Boycott
[f. the name of Capt. Boycott, an Irish
landlord, who was the original victim of
the treatment described.]
(*Oxford English Dictionary*)
*Captain Charles Cunningham Boycott
was the land agent for Lord Erne in Mayo.
In 1880, his tenants rebelled against their
oppressive and unjust treatment by with-
drawing their labour.*

brag noun and verb, 'arrogant, boastful
language'
G: *bréag*, 'lie, deception'
E: etymology uncertain
*Caesar's Thrasonical brag of I came, saw,
and ouercome.*
(Shakespeare, *As You Like It*, Act V,
Scene ii)

brake noun, 'clump of bushes'
G: *breac-choill*, 'straggling wood'
E: etymology uncertain
*He saw again the cane brakes and
cypresses of gliding plantations.*
(Harriet B. Stowe, *Uncle Tom's Cabin*)

brat noun, 'shawl, child'
G: *brat*, 'cloak, mantle, shawl'
E: etymology uncertain
*The shift in meaning from 'container' to
'contained' is not uncommon. We find it
also, for example, in* **bardicks**, *'possess-
ions', from* **barrdóg**, *'pannier'.*

brehon noun, 'judge'
G: *breitheamh*, 'judge, who presided
over Brehon Law, the legal system
replaced by the English system in
the seventeenth century
*In the case of murder, the Brehon, that is
their judge, will compound between the
murderer and the friends of the party
murdered.*
(Edmund Spenser, *A View of the Present
State of Ireland*, 1596)

brogue noun, 'shoe'
G: *bróg*, 'shoe, boot'
*Kicking on the shins with the points of a
brogue or shoe …*
(William Carelton, 'The Hedge
School')

brogue noun, 'accent'
[*Deriv. unknown: from the frequent mention of 'Irish brogue', it has been conjec-
tured that this may be the same word as
the prec., as if 'the speech of those who
wear brogues', or 'who call their shoes
brogues'; but of this there is no evidence.*]
(*Oxford English Dictionary*)

bum noun and verb, 'loafer, cadge'
G: *bomann* 'boast, bluster'
E: etymology uncertain
He was probably bumming his way home.
(F. Scott Fitzgerald, *The Great Gatsby*)

bun(s) noun, 'posterior'
G: *bun*, 'stump, root, tail of a hare',
'bottom, base'

E: etymology unknown
They used to get money for collecting rabbit buns.

but conjunction
EI: *but*
She's a brave size but. (She's a big woman.)

C

cadge noun and verb, 'steal, beg'
G: *goid*, 'steal' (pronounced to rhyme with 'fudge')
E: etymology unknown
They had nothing so they had to cadge a bit of food.

cairn noun, 'monument made of stones'
G: *cam, cairn*, 'pile of stones, sacred to the Druids'
Do you notice that the M1's not straight just before you get to Dungannon? Well, there was a cairn on the straight line and the men were afraid to knock it down so the engineer had to go round it.

camogie noun, 'game like hurling played by women'
G: *camógaí*, 'player of camogie'
She was the captain of the camogie team when she was at school and she could swing thon stick like a good 'un.

cant noun and verb, 'manner of speaking associated with beggars'
G: *cainnt*, 'talk'
E: etymology uncertain, perhaps from Latin *cantare*, 'to sing'
Cant and vision are to the ear and the eye the same that tickling is to the touch.
(Jonathan Swift, *Tale of a Tub*)

caulcannon, colcannon noun, 'potatoes mashed with milk and butter and seasoned with cabbage or scallions or nettles'
G: *cál + ceannfhionn*, 'cabbage + white head'
Forester ... dined like a philosopher upon colcannon.
(Maria Edgeworth, *Moral Tales*)

ceili(dhe) noun, 'evening visit, social event with singing and dancing'
G: *céilidhe*
Is she still out on her ceilidhe?

champ noun, 'mashed potatoes with butter, milk and something green'
EI: *champ*, 'chew, mashed potatoes'
Champ's got very expensive now. You can get it in any of the big restaurants.

child voc., 'endearment to young person'
G: *a leanbh*, 'child, darling'
E: *child*
Come here, child. Take this and buy yourself a wee something.

clabar, clabber noun, 'mud'
G: *clábar*, 'mud'
An' I'm dyin' in Drumlister In clabber to the knee.
(W.F. Marshall, 'Me an' me Da')

clag, cleg noun, 'horsefly'
G: *cuileóg*, 'fly'
E: via Old Norse *kleggi*
The clags is bad the night. They'd eat you alive.

clan noun, family
G: *clann*, 'family'
They're all related through-other because they're really all the one big clan.

clannish adj., 'cliquish'
G: *clann*, 'family'
The Magees were always clannish.

clash verb, 'tell tales, gossip'
EI: *clash*, 'gossip'
The mair they talk I'm kent the better,
E'en let them clash.
(Robert Burns, 'Welcome to an
Illegitimate Child')

clashbag noun, 'telltale'
EI: *clash*, 'gossip'
We called them 'clashbags' in my day.
They tried to be the teacher's pet by
clashin' on us but they always got the first
crack of a new cane.

clock noun, 'beetle'
G: etymology uncertain, perhaps from
    cuileóg, 'fly'
E: etymology uncertain
The clocks crawl in; the clocks crawl out.
They crawl in thin but they crawl out
stout ...
(Children's song)

clock noun, 'bell, timepiece'
Old Irish: *cloc*, 'bell'
E: etymology uncertain
In both [Coptic and Celtic Christianity]
the handbell played a very prominent place
in ritual, so much so that in early Irish
sculpture clerics are distinguished from lay
persons by placing a clochette in their
hand.
(William Dalrymple, *From the Holy*
Mountain)

cod noun and verb, 'trick, fool'
G: *cadach*, 'humbug, tomfoolery'
E: etymology unknown
Would you quit your coddin'? Couldn't
you be sensible for five minutes?

cog verb, 'copy, cheat by using someone
else's work'
G: *caog*, 'wink at'
E: etymology unknown
Out-facing, fashion-mongring boyes,
That lye, and cog, and flout, depraue, and
slander.
(Shakespeare, *Much Ado about Nothing*)

colleen noun, 'young woman'
G: *cailín*, 'unmarried woman'
Your young colleen bawn, that 'ill be your
wife before the sun sets.
(William Carleton, 'Shane Fadh's
Wedding')

cop, cap noun and verb, 'stop, seize,
think'
G: *ceap*, 'stop, seize, think'
E: etymology uncertain
Cap that calf.

coracle, curach, curragh noun, 'small
wickerwork boat covered with hides or
other waterproof material'
G: *curach*, 'small boat'
I believe 'coracle' is the correct word for
them wee boats but we always called them
'curachs'.

crack noun and verb, 'joke, enjoyment,
lively conversation'
G: *cracaire*, 'jester', *craic*, 'conversation'
E: etymology uncertain
Having had another crack with the old man.
(H.D. Thoreau, *Cape Cod*)

creel, kreel noun, 'wickerwork basket
for carrying turf'
G: *críol*, 'wickerwork basket'
The wet turf was a gift from your father to
the school, a whole kreel of it ...
(Edna O'Brien, A *Pagan Place*)

crooskeen, cruiscin noun, 'small jug'
G: *crúiscín*, 'small jug or pot'

There he is … in his gloryhole [small, dark cupboard], *with his cruiskeen lawn* [full jug of whiskey] *and his load of papers …*
(James Joyce, *Ulysses*)

cuddle noun and verb, 'hug, embrace'
G: etymology uncertain, perhaps from *codalta*, 'sleeping'
E: etymology unknown
Give us a wee cuddle then before you go to bed.

culchee, culchie noun, 'someone from the back of beyond'
G: etymology uncertain, perhaps from *cultor dei* becoming 'culdee' or *coill-teach*, 'a wooded area'
He started to roar an' laugh an' said te the driver, we've got a right culchie here, Mick.
(Frances Molloy, *No Mate for the Magpie*)

Curmudgeon 'churlish person'
G: etymology uncertain, but perhaps related to *caime*, 'crookedness'
E: etymology unknown
Such a clownish Curmudgen.
(Richard Stanyhurst, *Treatise containing a Plaine and Perfect Description of Ireland*)

D

dag noun, 'unpleasant person', a "hard case"'
G: etymology uncertain, perhaps from *dáigh*, 'stubborn, obdurate'
E: etymology unknown
Five years ago he was a drunken dag and now he's one of the best set up men in the place.

dear noun, 'God'
G: *Dia*, 'God'
Dear knows but I rared an eejit!

destroyed adj. 'ruined, spoiled (of a child)'
G: *millte*, 'destroyed, ruined, spoiled'
E: *destroyed*
She has the child destroyed. He gets everything he can think of.

doubt verb, 'strongly suspect'
E: *suspect* (archaic)
IE: 'strongly suspect'
I doubt there'll be a thunderstorm soon. It's hot and clammy and the clouds are gathering.

drool verb, 'drivel, salivate'
G: etymology uncertain, perhaps from *dreolán*, 'foolish person'
E: etymology unknown
He has the odd wee dwam [turn], *you know, and then he drools a bit about when he was a child, but sure there's no harm in him. Most of the time, he's as good as gold.*

drownded adj., 'soaked to the skin'
G: *báidhte*, 'drownded, drenched, soaked'
E: *drowned*
Och, you're drownded, child. Come in and get them wet clothes off.

dud(h)een noun, 'clay pipe'
G: *dúidín*, 'short clay pipe'
He's lost his dudeen.
(Samuel Beckett, *Waiting for Godot*)

dudgeon noun, 'feeling of anger, resentment'
G: etymology uncertain, perhaps from *doid* + *ín*, 'closed fist + diminutive'
E: etymology uncertain
I hope you are not going out in dudgeon, cousin?
(William Congreve, *The Old Bachelor*)

dullice, dulse noun, 'edible seaweed'
G: *duileasg*, 'edible seaweed'

Did you treat your Mary-Anne
To some dullice and yellowman
At the Oul' Lammas Fair in
Ballycastle O?
(Traditional song)

E

eejit noun and verb, 'fool' but with
friendly overtones
EI: *idiot*
*I felt an eejit when I realised that I had no
money.*

eerie adj., 'weird'
SEE: **airy**

evening noun, 'after noon'
G: *tráthnóna*, 'time of nones' (the ninth
 hour of the Roman day, ie, 3pm)
E: *evening*
*Why don't you come round in the early
evening. Come about one.*

ever adv., courteous intensifier
G: *ar bith*, 'at all', *i bhfad* and *riamh*, 'ever'
E: *ever*
*Would you ever have a pen on you? Mine's
run out.*

F

fake noun, 'appearance', 'cancer' in the
expression 'the quare fake'
G: *féach*, 'look'
E: etymology uncertain
*There was always a terrible fear of cancer.
People wouldn't utter the word without
saying 'God forbid!' or they'd call it 'the
quare fake'.*

farl noun, 'home-made bread'
EI: *fardel*, 'fourth part of a thin cake'
*Special Today: Soda Farls and Treacle
Farls*
(Sign in supermarket)

Fenian noun, 'Republican or Republi-
can sympathiser'
G: *fianna*, 'warriors'
*Some died by the wayside, some died by the
stranger,
And wise men have told us their cause was
a failure,
But they loved dear old Ireland and never
feared danger
Glory O glory O to the bold Fenian men.*
(Traditional song)

fey adj., 'gifted with second sight'
G: *feic*, 'a spectacle'
E: *fey*, 'fated to die'
*The mother was fey. She could read the cups
as well as you or me could read the paper!*

fire verb, 'throw'
G: *caith*, 'throw, shoot'
E: *fire*
*They were firing stones at the barracks,
but they hit nothing. Them boys couldn't
fire goats' pills.*

friend noun, 'relative'
G: *cara*, 'friend, relative'
E: *friend*
We were friends through-other, you see.
(W.F. Marshall, 'Sarah Anne')

G

galluses noun, 'braces'
EI: plural of *gallows*
*Don't forget your galluses or you'll make
an exhibition of yourself.*
(John Pepper, *Ulster-English Dictionary*)

galoot noun, 'rough person, usually a
man'
G: *gealt*, 'madman, lunatic'
E: etymology unknown
*He could lam[beat] any galoot of his
inches in America.*
(Mark Twain, *Innocent at Home*)

galore adj., 'in plenty, lots of'
G: *go leór*, 'lots of'
They had money galore in them days.

get ... death verb, 'die'
G: *bás a fháil*, die (death to get)
E: *get ... death*
I ... told him he would get his death in the rain.
(James Joyce, *Dubliners*)

glug noun and verb, 'gurgling noise, gurgle'
G: *gliogar*, 'rattle, empty noise'
E: etymology uncertain, perhaps echoic
There's a gluggin' in me guts. A bite hasn't passed my lips since morning.

gob, gub noun, 'mouth'
G: *gob*, 'beak, snout'
Biddy fetched her a belt on the gob.
('Finnegan's Wake', song)

gorb noun, 'glutton'
G: *carball*, 'palate, roof of dog's mouth'
E: etymology unknown
He's a gorb. He'd never say he'd had enough.

great adj, 'friendly'
G: *go mór*, 'great, friendly'
E: *great*
They've been very great since they were children.

guff noun, 'cheek, empty words'
G: *giofacht*, 'officiousness'
E: etymology unknown
You can't run them on patriotic songs ... and guff and bugaboo.
(G.B. Shaw, *The Apple Cart*)

gunk noun and verb, 'shock, disappointment'
G: *geangadh*, 'beating, mauling'

E: *gunk*, 'type of detergent'
I got the quare oul' gunk when he didn't show up.

H

hack noun, 'worn-out horse'
G: *each*, 'horse'
E: abbreviated from *hackney*, possibly from Old French, *haquenée*, 'an ambling horse or mare'
A good hack now would set you back a lock of hundred (i.e several hundred pounds).

hobo noun, 'wandering workman, itinerant'
G: etymology uncertain, perhaps from *ob*, 'fail, reject, shun'
E: etymology unknown
The gillies have ... gathered in some wretched hobo they found looking at the river.
(John Buchan, *John Macnab*)

hooker noun, 'wooden craft with sails'
EI: *hooker*, 'ship'
Dutch: *hoeker*, 'fishing boat'
... the hooker's tacking from the east.
(J.M. Synge, *Riders to the Sea*)

hooley noun, 'cheerful party'
G: perhaps from *céilí*, 'evening visit, party'
E: etymology unknown
... for there's a hooley on in Hannigan's house tonight.
(Song)

hooligan noun, 'rough person'
G: *Ó h-Uallacháin*, 'O'Houlihan'
There's hooligans in all walks of life.

hot-press noun, 'cupboard above or enclosing a hot-water tank, airing cupboard'
EI: *press*, 'cupboard'
Put them wet things in the hot-press. They'll be bone dry by morning.

hug noun and verb, 'warm embrace'
G: *cuaich*, 'embrace warmly' as in *chuaich sí a leanbh'*. (In the past tense the pronunciation is 'hoo+ich'.)
E: etymology unknown
Veiled Prophet, Faith, fanatic Faith, once wedded fast
To some dear false-hood, hugs it to the last.
(Thomas Moore, *Lalla Rookh*)

hump verb, 'carry or shift a heavy object'
G: *iompar*, 'carry'
E: etymology unknown
You may hump them blocks yourself for nobody asked you to put them there.

hungry grass noun, 'grass that is supposed to make those who walk on it hungry'
G: *féar gorta*, 'hungry grass'
He is eating as if he had trodden on the hungry grass.
(W.B. Yeats, *Mythologies*)

hurl noun and verb, 'fling, throw'
G: Irish game of *hurley* or *hurling*
E: etymology uncertain
Sometimes one barony hurls against another, but a marriageable girl is always the prize.
(Arthur Young, *Tour in Ireland*, 1780)

hurley noun, 'game played with a curved stick and a ball, similar to hockey'
SEE: **hurl** above

Hurley is a great game to watch. It's fast but it can be dangerous but.

hush noun and verb, 'quiet'
G: *Bí i do thost*, 'be quiet' (*thost* is pronounced like 'hust')
We'll have a bit of hush now, please.

I

ignorant adj., 'unmannerly, rude'
EI: *ignorant*, 'unmannerly'
He's worse than bad-mannered. He's an ignorant plug!

inchland noun, 'marshland'
G: *inis*, 'island'
E: *land*
Land's got out of all buying – even inchland.

in it preposition phrase, 'alive, in existence'
G: *ann*, 'in it, in existence'
E: *in it*
…we wouldn't see him want anything while he was in it.
(James Joyce, *Dubliners*)

J

jig noun, 'lively dance or music for the dance'
G: *dígeann*, 'climax'
E: etymology uncertain
The Irish jig, which they can dance with a most luxuriant expression.
(Arthur Young, *Tour in Ireland*, 1780)

jockey noun, 'professional rider of horses'
G: *eachaí*, 'horseman'
E: Jock + y, pet form of 'Jock'
The owner told Clarence the clocker. The clocker told jockey Magee.

The jockey, of course, passed it on to the horse,
And the horse told me.
(Song)

K

keen, keeny verb, 'lament, wail'
G: *caoin*, 'cry', *caoineadh*, 'crying'
I won't care what way the sea is when the other women will be keening.
(J.M. Synge, *Riders to the Sea*)

kern noun, 'Irish foot soldier'
G: *ceithern*, 'band of soldiers'
Now for our Irish wars,
We must supplant those rough rug-headed Kerns
(Shakespeare, *Richard II*)

kibosh, kybosh noun, 'end'
G: *caip an bháis*, 'death cap'
E: etymology uncertain
The Rector pull'd out an' oul' fourpinny-bit … An' handed the pill that wid kibosh the fun.
('Cruck-a-Leaghan' & 'Slieve Gallion', *Lays and Legends of the North of Ireland*, 1884)

kish noun, 'rush basket'
G: *cis*, 'wickerwork basket'
My mother could make kishes and they were the quare mark for carrying turf.

L

lag noun, 'no-hoper, convict'
G: *lag*, 'weak, weak person', perhaps reinforced by *leagaire*, 'wrestler'
E: etymology unknown
They were lags and spongers all of them.

lashings noun, 'large quantities'
EI: *lashings*, 'great amounts'
It was a great do. There was lashings and leavings!

leery adj., 'wary'
G: etymology uncertain, perhaps from *léire*, 'clear-headedness'
E: etymology uncertain
You'd need to be leery when you're dealing with the men in Petticoat Lane. They'd sell you stuff that you'd never buy if you had your senses about you!

leprechaun noun, 'short fairy man, who mends shoes and has a purse full of gold'
G: *leipreachán*, 'fairy man'
In a shady nook one moonlit night, a leprechaun I spied
With scarlet cap and coat of green, a crooskeen [jug of liquor] by his side.
(Traditional song)

liss noun, 'fort, fairy fort'
G: *lios*, 'circular fort'
Him who drove the gods out of their liss.
(W.B. Yeats, 'Secret Rose')

loch, lock noun, 'few'
G: *loca*, 'handful, small quantity'
E: *lock*, 'lock of hair, handful'
I only wanted a lock of eggs and it didn't seem worth my while to go to the shops for that.

loch, lough noun, 'lake'
G: *loch*, lake
They say there's a townland under Lough Neagh.

(me) lone adj., 'alone'
G: *mé féin*, 'myself', *tú féin* 'yourself'
E: *lone*
I'm tired sitting me lone of a night and she's not much better for she's her lone too most nights.

lore noun, 'information, teaching'
G: *leabhar*, 'book' (pronounced like 'lyore')

Green English

E: *lore*
Well, there's fairy-lore and there's plant-lore and people are forgetting both.

M

machree, mochree endearment, 'my love, beloved'
G: *mo chroí, 'my heart, my love'*
Thanks to you, little Molly – cuishla ma chree, pulse of my heart.
(Mrs Gaskell, *Wives and Daughters*)
SEE: **acushla**

marya(h), how are ya negative phrase, 'as it were, as if'
G: *mar dheadh, 'as it were'*
Is he sleeping? He is, marya!
He has money how are ya!

mass, meas noun, 'respect, regard'
G: *meas, 'regard, esteem'*
She has no mass at all in fancy clothes.

mavourneen noun, 'my love'
G: *mo mhúirnín, 'my little darling'*
Hush, mavourneen, don't cry.
(H. Jay, *Connaught Cousins*)

meskin noun, 'crock, crock of butter'
G: *meascán, 'pat of butter, small dish'*
They don't make meskins now, but they were the quare mark after churning.

mitch verb, 'play truant'
EI: *mitch, 'play truant'*
The girls hardly ever mitch or skive.

muck noun, 'mud'
G: *muc, 'pig'*
E: *muck, 'cattle dung'*
She observed, that 'by the living jingo, she was all of a muck of sweat'.
(Oliver Goldsmith, *The Vicar of Wakefield*)

N

neggin, noggin, naggin noun, 'quantity of liquor'
G: *noigín, 'small container'*
E: etymology unknown
They had a couple of five-neggin bottles of whiskey and a drop or two of brandy but that was about all. It was a very dry wake.

nor conjunction, 'than'
G: *ná, 'than'*
E: etymology obscure, perhaps reduction of *nother*
She's older nor any of us.

O

och interjection, 'och, but'
SEE: **ach**

ogham noun, 'type of alphabet'
G: *ogham, 'type of alphabet'*
The ogham alphabet used straight lines to represent sounds. According to legend, it was invented by Ogma to provide a means of recording secrets.

old-fashioned adj., 'precocious'
EI: *She was only four but she was as cute as a fox and as old-fashioned as a young woman.*

oxther noun, 'armpit'
EI: *oxter, 'armpit'*
Under his oxther he stuck it and away on up the hill.

oxther-cog verb, 'go arm in arm'
SEE: above
They may be fighting the day, but they'll be oxther-coggin the morrow.

P

pad noun, 'path'
EI: *pad*, 'path'
*The oul' dog for the hard road and the pup
for the pad.*
(Proverb)

pishogue noun, 'superstitious belief,
charm, spell'
G: *piseog*, 'charm, spell'
Little people, pishogues, leprechauns.
(R. Kipling, *Puck of Pook's Hill*)

pitter, pratie, pretty noun, 'potato'
G: *prataí*, 'potatoes'
E: *potato*
*You're welcome to the garden where the
praties grow.*
(Song)

planter noun, 'outsider'
EI: *planter*, term given to the
seventeenth-century English and
Scottish settlers in Ireland
*They're not local. They're planters. I
believe the father's people came from
Dumfries a couple of hundred years ago.*

playboy noun, 'person not to be trusted'
EI: *playboy*, 'wealthy pleasure seeker'
*You're the walking playboy of the western
world.*
(J.M. Synge, *Playboy of the Western World*)

pluck noun, 'courage'
G: *pluc*, 'cheek, bulge'
E: *pluck*, 'tug, jerk, pull out'
*Cissy Caffery bent over him to tease his fat
little plucks …*
(James Joyce, *Ulysses*)

poke noun, 'bag, sack, ice-cream cone'
G: *póca*, 'pocket, container'
E: etymology uncertain
You used to go into Miss Rogers and get a
*pennyworth of sweets in a wee paper poke.
Two sliders [ice-cream in wafers] and
one poke, please.*

pooka noun, 'sprite, hobgoblin'
G: *púca*
*The Pooka … seems essentially an animal
spirit.*
(W.B. Yeats, *Fairy and Folk Tales of
Ireland*)

poteen noun, 'illicitly brewed alcohol'
G: *poitín*, 'little pot, moonshine, illicit
whiskey'
*Poteen – poteen – poteen. Even if I did
speak Irish, I'd always be an outsider
here …*
(Brian Friel, *Translations*)

puck noun, 'goat'
G: *poc*, 'male goat'
*They put a goat up on a pole at Puck Fair
and everybody danced round and honoured it.*

puck noun, 'blow, punch'
G: *poc*, 'sharp blow'
*Well, the oul' one she gave him a puck on
the jaw.*

puke noun and verb, 'obnoxious per-
son, vomit'
G: *piachán*, 'hoarseness'
E: etymology unknown
*Thon puke should catch himself on. He's
as ignorant as he's educated.*

puss noun, 'face'
G: *pus*, 'lip, grimace'
*She's sitting in there with a puss on her
because she didn't get out last night.*

Q

quare adj. and adverb, 'odd, strange,
very'
EI: *queer*, 'odd'

The Quare Fellow *is a play by Brendan Behan.*
She's quare'n handy in the kitchen.

R

rag noun, 'temper'
G: *ráig*, 'sudden outbreak'
She's a lovely girl but she can lose her rag very quick.

rann noun, 'verse'
G: *rann*, 'quatrain, stanza'
Know, that I would accounted be
True brother of a company
That sang to sweeten Ireland's wrong,
Ballad and story, rann and song.
(W.B. Yeats, 'To Ireland in the Coming Times')

rath noun, 'fairy ring fort, rampart'
G: *ráth*, 'earthen rampart, ring fort'
There is a great use amongst the Irish to make greate assemblyes togither upon a rath or hill.
(Edmund Spenser, *A View of the Present State of Ireland*, 1596)

reel noun and verb, 'lively dance', 'whirl round'
G: *ríl*, 'dance'
E: etymology obscure
She won the championship with her last dance, the reel.

S

sally noun, 'willow'
G: *saileach*, 'willow'
E: *sallow*, 'willow'
You were sent to find a sally wattle and when you brought it in, you always got the first slap with it. Sallies could give you a quare welt.

In the olive darkness of the sally-trees
Silently moved the air.
(J. Wright, *Woman to Man*)

sancy, sonsy adj., 'healthy, pretty, attractive'
G: *sonasach*, 'happy, healthy'
She's as sancy a wee blade as ever you clapped eyes on.

scrab noun and verb, 'scratch'
G: *screab*, 'scum, crust'
E: *scrape*
Look at the scrab that cat of yours gave me.

shannach noun and verb, 'chat'
G: *seanchas*, 'traditional wisdom'
Many's the right shannach I had in Eileen's, God rest her.

shanty noun, 'small house'
G: *seantigh*, 'old house'
E: etymology uncertain
I am the little Irish boy
That lives in the shanty.
(H.D. Thoreau, *Journal*, Nov. 26, 1850)

shebeen noun, 'place where unlicenced liquor is sold'
G: *síbín*, 'illicit drinking establishment'
Well first we reconnoitred round O'Sullivan's Shebeen …
('Slattery's Mounted Foot')
[He]*spends his last night in the Colony drunk, and by chance encounters his dark love in some shabby Shebeen.*
(Doris Lessing, *Golden Notebook*)

sheeog(u)e noun, 'fairy, changeling'
G: *sí* + *óg*, 'young fairy'
That's not me da ye'r makin' all this fuss about, a said, that's a sheeoge.
(Frances Molloy, *No Mate for the Magpie*)

shenanigans noun, 'tricks, mischief'
G: *sionnachaigh*, 'play the fox'
E: etymology uncertain
You can't be up to them, them or their shenanigans!

shindig noun, 'lively party, get together'
G: *sínteach*, 'generous'
E: etymology uncertain
We're all invited to the shindig they're throwing.
'What's a ceilidh anyway?'...
'It's Gaelic for a gathering, a shindig.'
(Colleen McCullough, *The Thorn Birds*)

shooler, shuiler noun, 'wanderer, hobo'
G: *siubhlóir*, 'walker'
Then when the shuiler begs,
Be neither hard nor cold:
The share that goes for Christ
Will come a hundredfold.
(Joseph Campbell, 'Every Shuiler is Christ')

shough, shuch noun, 'drain, ditch'
G: *sruth*, 'stream, river'
E: *sough*, 'boggy place'
Sometimes one in crossing a stile or ditch would drop into the shough.
(William Carleton, *Traits and Stories of the Irish Peasantry*)

slane noun, 'type of spade for cutting turf'
G: *sleán*, turf spade
There isn't a spade-load of good slane turf.
(J. Barlow, *Irish Idylls*)

slob noun, 'slovenly person'
G: *slaba*, 'mud, ooze, slovenly person'
A heavy-looking poor slob of a man.
(A.H. Clington, *Frank O'Donnell*)

slogan noun, 'dictum, motto, axiom'
G: *sluagh ghairm*, 'battle cry'
The somewhat disingenuous slogan of 'ban the bomb'.
(Harold Macmillan, *Riding the Storm*)

slug noun and verb, 'mouthful, gulp'
G: *slog*, 'swallow'
E: etymology uncertain
Give us a slug of that lemonade. I've a terrible druth on me.

smidgeon, smidgin noun, 'tiny amount'
G: *smiodar* + *ín*, 'little piece, fragment'
E: etymology uncertain
You little, silly, half-pint, smidgin of a wife.
(John Steinbeck, *East of Eden*)

smithereens noun, 'tiny little bits'
G: *smidirín*, 'little fragments'
... flipping the sky
Into smithereens.
(Seamus Heaney, 'May')

so long phrase, 'goodbye'
G: *slán*, 'safety', used in phrase *slán agat*, meaning 'goodbye'
E: etymology uncertain
I whisper So long! And take the young woman's hand ... for the last time.
(Walt Whitman, *Poems*)

spags noun, 'very sensible shoes'
G: *spág*, 'foot, hoof, claw'
She wasn't at a dance in spags? ... Sure nobody would be that daft.

spalpeen noun, 'farm labourer'
G: *spailpín*, 'itinerant farm labourer'
You wouldn't call anybody a spalpeen now. It's a bit like 'navvy'. It's not what you'd like to be called.

spree noun and verb, 'boisterous activity, drinking bout'
G: *spré*, 'scatter, squander'

E: etymology uncertain

*I've longed for to be a man to go spreeing,
even if it were only a tramp to some new
place in search o' work.*
(Mrs Gaskell, *North and South*)

spud noun, 'potato'
G: *spadar*, 'clod, sodden turf'
E: etymology uncertain
*I'm fond of a spud now. I wouldn't feel full
if I didn't have my spuds every day.*

spunk noun, 'courage, spirit'
G: *sponc*, 'tinder, courage, mettle'
E: etymology uncertain
The squire has got spunk in him.
(Oliver Goldsmith, *She Stoops to
Conquer*)

store, noun, 'treasure'
G: *stór*, 'treasure'
E: *store*, 'container'
*She is my store, oh she is my store,
Whose grey eye wounded me so sore.*
(Douglas Hyde, *Lovesongs of Connacht*)

T

taig, teague noun, 'Catholic'
G: *Tadhg*, 'Tim'
*This week a new slogan appeared along the
Shankill Road, the backbone of Protestant
West Belfast. It read: 'All Taigs are tar-
gets.'*
(*Observer*, 31 October, 1982)

take soup phrase, 'become a Protestant
for a mercenary motive'
E: *take + soup*, influenced by Irish
    experience
*They say they used to give pauper children
soup to become protestants [sic] in the time
of the potato blight.*
(James Joyce, *Ulysses*)

teem verb, 'to pour with rain, be
prolific'
G: *taom*, 'to empty of water, bail'
E: *teem*, 'rain, empty a vessel, be
    prolific'
It was teeming out of the heavens!

through-other adj. and adv., 'confused,
mixed up'
G: *tré na chéile*, 'untidy' (lit. through its
    spouse or mate)
E: *through + other* influenced by
*The house was through-other but the
welcome was warm.*

trouble noun, 'death in a family'
E: *trouble*, reinforced by the Irish
    expression 'to be sorry for your
    trouble'
*I'm sorry for your trouble, Mary, but it
was a peaceful end he had.*

Troubles noun, 'period of violence in
Ireland from 1916–23', and 'period of
violence in Northern Ireland since
1969'
E: *troubles*, modified by Irish usage
This is Ireland of the Troubles …
(Seán O'Casey, introducing *Juno and the
Paycock*)

trousers noun, 'pants'
G: *triúas*, 'trews, trousers'
*Deedle, deedle dumpling, my son John,
Went to bed with his trousers on.
One shoe off and one shoe on,
Deedle, deedle dumpling, my son John.*
(Children's rhyme)

twig verb, 'understand'
G: *tuig*, 'understand'
E: etymology unknown
*Do you twig what I'm saying, or do I have
to spell it out?*
(James Joyce, *Dubliners*)

U

uilleann pipes noun phrase, 'pipes played by squeezing the bellows with the elbow'
G: *uilleann*, 'elbow'
Is it hard to play uilleann pipes?
Well, it's hard to listen to them if you don't play them right.

unbeknownst adj. and adv., 'unknown'
EI: *unbeknownst*
Burying your poor father unbeknownst when ... we could have given him a decent burial.
(J.M. Synge, *Playboy of the Western World*)

W

wake noun and verb, 'ritual vigil by relatives and friends after a death, often a period of reminiscing associated with the dead person'
E: *wake*, preserved in Ireland
In Ireland, the sleep that knows no waking is followed by the wake that knows no sleeping.
(Common aphorism)

wee adj., 'small, young'
EI: *wee*
His wee blade [young daughter] *is getting married on Saturday.*

wheaten bread noun phrase, 'home-made bread'
E: *wheaten* + *bread*, preserved in Ireland
Wheaten bread's filling now, especially when it's still warm.

wheen noun, 'several'
EI: *wheen*, 'not many'
We haven't had sunshine like this in a wheen of Sundays!
SEE: **lock**

whenever conj., 'when'
EI: *whenever*, 'when'
Mix the butter and sugar and whenever it's creamy, add the flour.

whin noun, 'furze'
EI: *whin*, 'furze'
Between small, whin-tough hills...
(John Montague, 'Home Again')

whinge verb, 'cry and moan, complain'
EI: *whinge*, 'whine, complain peevishly'
You crossed her last wish in death and yet you sulk with me because I don't whinge like some hired mute from Lalouette's.
(James Joyce, *Ulysses*)

whisht noun and exclamation, 'silence'
G: *Bí i do thost*, 'be quiet'
Would you houl' your whisht. I can't hear my ears.
SEE: **hush**

whiskey noun, 'spiritous liquor'
G: *uisce beatha*, 'water of life'
O, whiskey, you're the devil
You're leading me astray,
Over hills and valleys
And to Americay ...
(Traditional song)

whisper noun, 'rumour'
G: *cogar*, whisper, hint
E: *whisper*
I got a whisper of it yesterday, but it's not common knowledge but.

wild adv., 'exceptionally'
G: *fiáin*, wild, intensely eager
E: *wild*
It was wild funny!

wrapped, rapt adj.'enraptured, deeply in love'
G: *dúnta i ngrá*, 'enclosed, fastened in love'

EI *rapt*, 'enraptured'
*She was wrapped in thon boy an' then he
up and left her.*

Y

yahoo noun, 'person who doesn't know
how to behave'
E: *yahoo*, term invented by Jonathan
   Swift
*The Fore-feet of the Yahoo differed from
my Hands in nothing else, but the Length
of the Nails, the Coarseness and Brown-
ness of the Palms, and the Hairiness
on the Backs.*
(Jonathan Swift, *Gulliver's Travels*,
1726)

yarra, yerra, arrah, interjection, 'God'
G: *a Dhia ara*, 'God'
*Yerra, sure the little hop-o'-my-thumb has
forgotten all about it.*
(James Joyce, *Dubliners*)

yeer possessive adj., 'your plural'
E: ye + 'r' (cf 'you' and 'your', 'they'
   and 'their')
Ye're all invited for yeer Christmas dinner.

yoke noun, 'thingamajig'
E: *yoke* but given an Irish meaning
*Yoke; any article, contrivance, or appara-
tus for use in some work. 'That's a quare
yoke Bill,' says a countryman when he first
saw a motor car.*
(P.W. Joyce, *English as we Speak it in
Ireland*)

your man noun phrase, 'a specified
person'
G: *do dhuine*, 'your person'
E: *your man*
Your man was delighted for a few hours.
(Brendan Behan, *The Quare Fellow*)

youse, yiz pronoun, 'you plural'
G *sibh*, 'you plural'
E: *you*
*Youse is all right. Youse can stay in. It's us
that has to go out.*

Index